The Accidental Bird Dog

The Accidental Bird Dog

Published by Terry Ann Fernando
Raleigh, North Carolina
www.accidentalbirddog.com

Library of Congress Control Number: 2024908864

ISBN (paperback): 979-8-218-44809-7

The Accidental Bird Dog

My Journey with an Extraordinary Vizsla

Terry Ann Fernando

"It is good to have an end to journey towards; but it is the journey that matters, in the end."

Ursula K. Le Guin

Table of Contents

Preface

Ten years ago, I had no interest in getting a dog. Every time my then-boyfriend, Chris, brought up the idea, I scoffed and tried to change the subject. *What did we need a dog for?* All I could think of was the tireless work and extra responsibility. But sooner than I imagined, my world was transformed with the introduction of a Vizsla puppy named Zara. Full of life from the start, she quickly changed my priorities.

I first thought about writing this book in the fall of 2019. I've always enjoyed writing, and recently I had completed a draft of an unrelated novel (which has yet to be published). By this point, I had already come quite a long way with Zara, and I knew I wanted to write a book about her some day. But I wasn't sure what I wanted it to be about. As I researched the genre of memoir, the idea became clear. Successful memoirs focus on one specific event or a series of events that change the course of the author's life. I would write a book about my journey training Zara for hunting events.

I started writing the manuscript in April 2020 during the COVID-19 lockdown. It seemed like the ideal time to get started, even though our training was still in progress. Zara was six-and-a-half then, so I knew it would take me some time to get the back story down, and I could figure out the rest later. I did not know how our journey or the book would end when I began, but she had already impacted my life enough that I knew it would be worthwhile to document. I wrote the bulk of it over the course of a year, although it's taken me several years since to refine and edit. Most of it was pretty easy to write, since I was recounting things that happened. Some names and identifying details have been changed in certain instances, but I have tried to be as true to events as my memory allows.

Zara and I have been on a remarkable journey. Sometimes it still seems incredible how far we've come. It's hard to describe how completely my life and sense of identity has changed in the past 10 years. Before, I had zero interest in hunting. I was completely freaked out by guns. I had never shot a gun at a range or sporting clays course. Hunting was simply another world, and it seemed outdated and old-fashioned to me. Growing up, I knew that my grandfather had hunted from the snippets of stories my dad told, and my uncle hunted deer and ducks. Even so, it wasn't even on my radar as an activity I could enjoy. I also had no experience training dogs, other than teaching my childhood dogs how to sit and lay down. I didn't know dog sports existed.

Now, there is literally no place I'd rather be than running in a field trial or walking through the woods with Zara hunting wild birds. My excitement over a weekend away for one of these excursions, let alone a bigger event, is unmatched. I am like a kid waiting for Christmas in anticipation.

Competing with Zara taught me that it's okay to fail. Before, I was a perfectionist and afraid of failure.

Zara, on the other hand, was not afraid of failure. And she certainly did not care about how other people perceived her. She charged headfirst into the unknown—be it thick brush, deep water, or an unfamiliar field trial course. She was not afraid to make mistakes either—even as she got more experienced and the rules for the bird dog game became more stringent. Her love of birds would overrule sometimes, and she'd take a step or a hop despite the threat of correction. She'd accept the consequence and move on. It did not deter her desire.

Whereas I had lacked confidence competing by myself in 10Ks or triathlons in my pre-dog life, in bird dog events, Zara gave me the strength I needed to push through and succeed. We were a team, and I couldn't let her down. Most of the time, she held up her end of the bargain. Therefore the bar was set high, and I strove to meet it.

The first few failures we experienced felt outsized in my mind. I took them hard. Eventually, the more we failed, the more I realized that the world was not ending. The failures became learning experiences and opportunities to share with others. And while that seems obvious, it took me a long time to take it to heart and understand that there was not a direct correlation between failing a test and me being a failure. Honestly, it's still something I'm working on.

I realize that my story might seem somewhat unbelievable. There were many instances when we could have gone astray and hit a dead-end that we couldn't recover from. In fact, I seriously considered giving up a few times. Part of the reason I wrote this story was to inspire others in a similar position. You have a goal that seems impossible? Why not give it a shot? You never know where life will take you.

Even though the hunting world is still very much male-dominated, I've seen a noticeable increase in women getting into bird hunting and bird dog training in the past few years. Like me, this is often because they got a hunting dog and then got curious about the dog's innate talents. I think women sometimes need a little extra support when entering this space. I hope my book helps to offer that encouragement.

The process of training my own dog has been incredibly satisfying and has taught me a lot about myself, hard work, success, and failure. Hunting and competing, for me and many of the people I'm surrounded with, is so much more than just shooting birds. It's about the bond you have with the dog, the joy in watching the dog work, and seeing your training pay off when your dog finally stands steady or retrieves a bird.

Lastly, I wanted to share how I became extremely passionate about something in which I previously had no interest. I think it can be unreasonable to expect that one day you'll just wake up super excited about something or know exactly what you want to do with your life. In Elizabeth Gilbert's book, *Big Magic*, she talks about finding a passion. You may not start out being enthusiastic about a particular thing or have any idea where it may lead. Instead, find something that sparks just a bit of interest in you and see where it goes.

Terry Ann Fernando
August 2024

Chapter 1

Why Do We Need a Dog?

Although people who know me now would be shocked to hear it, for a long time, I did not want a dog. I started dating my now-husband, Chris Fernando, in the summer of 2011. Fairly early on, he mentioned that he wanted a dog. I was dismissive. "Why do you want a dog?" I asked with disdain. "They're so much work."

We'd be walking down the street and pass a person with a dog (typically a large breed like a German Shepherd or Labrador Retriever), and he'd say wistfully, "That's a nice dog." I'd grunt or shrug my shoulders and try to change the subject.

I was not unfamiliar with dogs. In fact, I had grown up with them. My family and I had gotten a Beagle puppy, Penny, when I was 10. Like most kids, I had loved Penny and enjoyed playing with her, but she was not my main concern. She was ultimately my mom's dog. As I got older and progressed into my teenage years, Penny lived on the periphery of my life. I was preoccupied with school and extracurricular activities.

During the spring of my senior year of high school, Penny became sick with a mysterious ailment. She had to stay several nights at the emergency vet clinic and then passed away at the age of seven. It was the first time I'd seen my dad cry. My mother was devastated, because Penny was like her third child. I was sad, but quickly moved on. I was about to graduate and head to college, after all.

About eight months later, during the winter break of my freshman year of college, my parents decided to get another Beagle puppy, whom we named Dixie. To me, it felt like they were trying to reincarnate Penny. She had died less than a year before. Looking back, I can understand why they wanted and needed to get another dog. At the time, though, I thought Dixie was cute, but I never was as attached to her as I had been to Penny. I didn't live with my parents full-time anymore, so I only saw Dixie on breaks from school. College, my friends, and figuring out what I wanted to do with my life were my full focus.

For many years afterwards, I had little interest in dogs. I was not one of those people who would stop owners on the street to pet their dog, I did not coo over cute puppies, and I certainly had no patience for other people's stories about their dogs. To me, a dog was an accessory part of family life, something that was omitted from Christmas card photoshoots and walked when time allowed. I never imagined that a dog could take a central place in determining the course of my life, my interests, and my passion.

In February 2012, Chris and I moved in together. We shared a two-level condo in Fairlington, an older neighborhood in Arlington, Virginia. Around the same time, we started spending more time with another couple, Erin and Dave. Chris and Dave had been roommates when Chris first moved to the Washington, DC area after college. Erin and Dave had adopted a mixed-breed puppy the previous year. His name was Jax, and even I had to admit he was cute—small and brown with perky ears and a black muzzle.

Jax, unlike any of the other dogs I had known, was well-trained. It was a revelation to me. He didn't pull on the leash, bark incessantly, or steal food from the table. Any time he started to act up, Erin and Dave were on him instantly with a correction. Besides basic commands like sit and shake, my family never taught our Beagles how to behave. Being around Jax made me realize that it was possible to have a dog that was a pleasurable companion, not a nuisance.

In May 2012, Erin and Dave got married, and Jax was the ring bearer in their wedding. He marched down the aisle with confidence, wearing a black and white tuxedo jacket. It was adorable. After their wedding, they went on a honeymoon for a week, and Chris and I agreed to watch Jax. He wasn't much trouble at all. I came home at lunch from work to let him out for a few minutes, and in the evenings, we took him to the dog park or out running with us. He never touched any of our things, and he slept quietly in his crate at night.

Chris was still talking about getting a dog, especially now that we were settled into our apartment. I was slowly warming up to the idea, but the idea of a puppy was daunting to me. "I want a dog that comes pre-trained, like Jax," I joked. Jax had shown me what a nice dog could be like, but I knew that Erin and Dave had spent hours getting him to this point. I wasn't sure I was ready for that.

One night in August, Chris and I invited Erin and Dave over for dinner. When they arrived, they had just been to the dog park with Jax. They started raving about a dog they had seen at the park. "This dog was running around, and all of a sudden, it leaped over the four-foot fence surrounding the dog park! It was incredible!" Dave exclaimed.

"Wow," I said. "That is impressive."

"We asked the owner what kind of dog it was and he said it was a Veezsh-luh."

"A what?" we asked.

"A Veezsh-luh? I'd never heard of it either."

Curious, we all sat down in the living room to Google this strange dog breed. Chris quickly found information about the breed. It was spelled *Vizsla*, which is a Hungarian word.

"Look, here's a *Runner's World* magazine article about Vizslas," Chris said excitedly, as he studied his phone. The article described the top dog breeds for runners, and the Vizsla was listed as one of the best. It was described as a good trail-running dog, good in the heat, good for long runs, and good for paces faster than a seven minute per mile pace (very fast!). We were both runners, and Chris was interested in finding a dog that could run with us.

"This is the dog!" Chris exclaimed. "This is the dog we need!"

"I don't know," I said slowly. "They sound like they need a *lot* of exercise."

Chris read more characteristics about Vizslas. They are very intelligent, sweet, easy to train, and called "Velcro" dogs because they like to be near their owners at all times. Vizslas were originally bred in Hungary as hunting dogs for the royal families. They would spend their days hunting for birds with their owners following on horseback and their evenings curled up in their owners' beds.

"They are cute," I admitted. Their sleek, athletic bodies covered with rust-colored fur gave them a regal look. They seemed to know that they were associated with royalty.

"See?!" Chris said. "We need a Vizsla!"

I rolled my eyes. Erin and Dave smiled. "Aren't you glad we went to the dog park today?" Erin said. I laughed.

Chapter 2

Taking the Leap

C hris and I discussed getting a dog off and on for the next several months. I still wasn't completely convinced that I wanted one, but Chris was doing his best to persuade me. At the beginning of 2013, I started researching Vizsla breeders to learn more about the breed and figure out if it was right for us. I contacted several people in Virginia and Maryland, and eventually connected with Jane Baker, a first-time breeder who lived in Ashburn, Virginia with her two Vizslas, Caiya and Piros. Jane and I quickly realized we had several things in common. Not only were we both graphic designers, but she and Chris both worked for the same consulting firm! It seemed like it was meant to be.

I told Jane that Chris and I were considering a Vizsla puppy. We were looking for a dog that could run with us and do other active things, like hiking. Jane was planning to breed her female, Caiya, that summer when she came into heat. Puppies would be expected to go home around November or December. She invited us to come meet her and watch Caiya at a field trial in March. Field trials are competitive dog events that were developed as a way to assess a dog's hunting performance against other dogs. Caiya had a busy schedule of training and competing in field events. Neither Chris nor I had any experience hunting, and it was not something we had thought about doing with a future dog. Although we weren't interested in hunting, we agreed to come to the field trial to meet her.

Jane also sent us a three-page questionnaire to fill out about why we wanted a Vizsla puppy, what we were looking for in a puppy, and information about us, like the type of place we lived in. I didn't know it at the time, but this is a hallmark of a good breeder. They use a questionnaire like this to screen potential puppy buyers. Back then, I couldn't have told you the difference between a responsible breeder and a "backyard breeder" just looking to make money.

Reputable breeders of purebred dogs are looking to improve the breed and follow the Standard when they choose a male and female pair. The Standard is a written document that describes the looks and characteristics of each breed. For example, the beginning of the American Kennel Club Vizsla Standard reads: "General appearance: That of a medium-sized, short-coated, hunting dog of distinguished appearance and bearing."[1]

Reputable breeders also typically title their dogs in sports such as field trials, conformation, and obedience. They complete the recommended health testing (such as hip and elbow X-rays, thyroid tests, etc.) and tend to breed only once or twice a year. They are a resource for the life of the dog and will take back a dog at any time if the owners can't keep it anymore. I feel grateful that I stumbled upon someone like Jane who checked all the boxes for a reputable breeder.

In March, Chris and I drove an hour and 20 minutes to Sumerduck, Virginia, a tiny town in the middle of nowhere that contained a large wildlife management area (WMA) where the field trial was being held. We felt a little intimidated driving onto the property. Neither of us had ever been to an event like this before. The dirt road wound up and around a hill, and along it were huge campers and horse trailers, flanked by pickup trucks. Horses and dogs were staked out between the vehicles. The dogs all went into a frenzy of barking as we slowly drove past them.

Thankfully, we quickly located Jane and her husband, Michael. They were very friendly and showed us where Caiya and their older male, Piros, were staked out. There were plenty of other Vizslas there, too—the trial was put on by the Conestoga Vizsla Club, after all. Chris and I stayed for about an hour and asked Jane and Michael all sorts of questions.

We didn't end up watching Caiya or any of the other dogs compete that day, but I wonder what we would have thought had we stayed. At the time, we didn't have a good idea of how fast and far a Vizsla could

---

1 The full Vizsla standard is available at
   https://images.akc.org/pdf/breeds/standards/Vizsla.pdf

run. In a trial like that one, the dogs take off at breakneck speed as soon as they are released and run their hearts out for 30 minutes, hunting for birds. I think it would have been eye-opening for us to have watched even one brace of the field trial. Then, again, it may have scared us off, had we realized the athleticism of these dogs. Vizslas are not casual weekend warriors. They are the equivalent of the fervent ultrarunner who does 25 miles on a Tuesday just for fun.

After visiting the field trial, I found myself researching everything I could about Vizslas. Since they are not a common breed, there weren't too many places for me to find information about them. In early 2013, the world of dog Instagram was just getting started. Instead, I found an online forum called *VizslaTalk*, where people posted questions about their Vizslas, and other members answered. It was enlightening to learn about the nuances of the breed. I also spent time reading the blog *It's A Vizsla Thing*, written by a Vizsla owner who lived in the San Francisco Bay area. I enjoyed the personal stories she posted about her Vizsla, Captain.

I don't remember when the switch flipped in my brain from not wanting a dog to wanting one badly. I think it was more of a gradual thing, worn down over months and months. By the summer of 2013, like Chris, I also was convinced that we needed a Vizsla puppy. The wait seemed interminable. In early August, nearly a year after we'd found out what a Vizsla was, Caiya came into heat. I celebrated this milestone by telling everyone I knew. I'm sure my coworkers thought I was a bit crazy as I went around exclaiming that my future puppy's mother was in heat.

Once a female dog enters her heat cycle, there is a period of about a week when she is the most fertile. This is when breedings normally take place. It turned out that instead of traveling to Iowa, where the male dog (a sire named Bull) lived, Caiya was going to be artificially inseminated. Jane explained that Caiya was a nervous traveler, so she didn't want to run the risk of driving to Iowa and not having a live breeding work out. Instead, Bull's semen was shipped to Virginia, and Caiya was inseminated in a veterinary hospital.

Dogs are pregnant for about 60 days. Veterinarians typically confirm the pregnancy by doing an ultrasound about a month after the female was bred. Then, at the end of the pregnancy, an X-ray is performed to count the number of puppies and check if there are any issues. Caiya was due to have her puppies in early October, which meant that they would be ready to go home sometime in December.

Even though the waiting seemed to stretch out forever, the timing worked out well for Chris and me. Both of our sisters were getting married that fall. My sister, Allison, got married on September 28th in Pennsylvania, and Chris' sister, Chamarie, was married on October 5th in Sri Lanka, where Chris was born. After attending Allison's wedding, we flew to Sri Lanka less than a week later. We spent two weeks in Sri Lanka, and on the day that we were scheduled to fly back to the U.S., we got word that Caiya's puppies had been born. She'd had seven: three girls and four boys. I was ecstatic.

Over the next several weeks, I waited impatiently for Jane to post videos and photos of the puppies to her Facebook page. We didn't know which puppy would be ours, because Jane was planning on doing temperament testing when they were seven or eight weeks old. But I enjoyed watching the development and antics of all the puppies, exclaiming over their cuteness. Chris was interested in seeing the updates too, but was not quite as excited as I was, even though he had been the one who initially had wanted a dog.

Chris and I spent a lot of time debating about what we would name our puppy. I wanted something short, that had one or two syllables, and a name that was unique. I had a list of names that included Bella, Etta, Clover, Elfie, Haley, Zoe, and Maya. I found that I liked a lot of boy names better, but we knew we were getting a girl. We both agreed that Colombo would be a great name for a dog. Colombo, Sri Lanka was the city Chris had grown up in. But Colombo sounded like a boy's name, and Colomba just sounded weird. By early December, we had narrowed the names down to Bella, Maya, and Zoe. Chris didn't love any of them. It was back to the drawing board. I came across the baby-naming website Nameberry.com. It had thousands of names, organized in useful lists like Winter Names, Flower Names, and British Names.

I searched and searched. We were sitting opposite each other at our computers in the basement of our townhouse. We'd recently had to move across the neighborhood to a different property after our initial landlord had wanted to sell his place. Then I saw it: Zara. It was short, unique, and memorable. "What about Zara?" I asked. Chris looked at me. "I like it," he said.

I read the description. In Hebrew and Arabic, Zara means princess. "Princess," I scoffed. I loved the name Zara, but didn't agree with the meaning behind it. Princesses were tiny dogs that people carried around in their purses and wore frilly outfits. Our Vizsla was going to be an athletic animal, a runner, an outdoorsy pup—definitely not a princess.

I would be wrong about that, like so many things.

Chapter 3

Preparations

As the fall of 2013 went on, the litter of seven Vizsla puppies continued to grow, as did my excitement. I was finally ready to have a dog of my own, and I was also ready to document the adventure. The time I spent reading the *It's A Vizsla Thing* blog inspired me to start my own blog. As a graphic designer, it was easy for me to set up a *Zara the Vizsla* blog. I planned to write about my experiences raising Zara and being a first-time Vizsla owner. I had also recently gotten an Instagram account and started following several Vizsla owners. Back then, there were relatively few people with dog accounts on Instagram, but I loved seeing the photos people posted of their Vizslas. I felt like I knew them, even though we'd never met. I changed the name of my account to @zarathevizsla. Zara's publicity was ready to go. All I needed was to bring her home.

In early December, Jane invited all of the puppy owners to watch the temperament testing. It was held on a Saturday morning in an office building, where Jane had gained access and permission to hold the activity. Temperament testing is a practice that breeders perform to assess the characteristics of each puppy so they can make educated decisions to match them with the right family. They look at physical characteristics, energy level, trainability, hunting desire (depending on the breed), and other personality traits, such as the ability to recover from stress. The puppies were eight weeks old when Jane did the temperament testing. She had invited a friend who was familiar with Vizslas to do the evaluation. Since Jane had spent eight weeks with the litter, she was somewhat biased.

I thought temperament testing was a great idea and was excited to watch. Chris and I arrived at the office that Saturday morning and met several of the families who would have Zara's littermates. Jane had all of the puppies in a wire X-pen. An X-pen is a set of connecting panels that can be set up as a small fenced area. We were able to pick up the puppies and cuddle them while they were not being tested. She also had a large fenced-off area that was filled with objects: a tunnel, a toy fire hydrant, a balance board, a crinkly surface, and plenty of toys. One by one, each puppy would be placed in the testing area, and the woman who was evaluating them would observe and perform certain activities with them.

The first up was pink girl. The puppies were identified by the color of collar they wore. As soon as pink girl was placed in the testing area, she took off, shooting around the objects as fast as she could. There were several small toys made of real fur scattered around the area to give an indication of each puppy's prey drive and hunting desire. Pink girl grabbed one of the fur toys and romped around with it, refusing to give it to the evaluator. She was feisty and had twice as much energy as all of the other puppies. Several of the others carefully picked their way across the floor, slowly taking everything in. Purple boy was deemed very trainable, as he allowed the tester to guide him across the wobble board. He would be great with children, the woman remarked. Red girl seemed very stubborn, as she refused to look the tester in the eye when she held her on her back. She was also a bit slow to warm up to new things.

Chris and I had told the other owners that we were runners and were looking for a running partner. "Oh, you should get the pink girl," one of them said. "She has lots of energy!"

Chris and I looked at each other in slight horror. *That puppy seemed crazy!* Clearly she should go to a family who was going to hunt with her. We had our eyes on the red or teal girls, although we knew the choice was not really up to us.

We had also decided on her registered name. The litter would be registered with the American Kennel Club (AKC), and each puppy needed an "official" name in addition to their "call" name. With the help of my sister, we decided on Trailside's Tzar of Fairlington. Fairlington was the name of the neighborhood we lived in and I liked the play on words with "tzar" meaning "ruler." Since Zara meant princess, it seemed to fit. Trailside was Jane's kennel name. Kennel names are used as prefixes to official names.

Jane thanked us for attending the temperament testing and told us she would make her decisions in a few days. We went home and spent another four days waiting. Coincidentally, I had just quit my job and was planning on taking three weeks off over the holidays before I started my new position at the end of December. This seemed like the perfect opportunity to get our puppy off to the right start.

Finally, on December 11th, we were able to bring Zara home. Jane had chosen the red collar girl for us. She was the biggest of the girls, which appealed to Chris. He preferred larger dogs and was hoping that Zara would end up on the heavier side of the 40–55 pound weight range for female Vizslas. The pink collar girl had gone to a family in Texas who already had another Vizsla and was planning on training her for field trials. It sounded like a good fit to me. Jane said that our puppy didn't seem to have strong hunting instincts. To further test the puppies' prey drive, Jane had brought a pigeon with a string attached to its foot into her garage. The string would keep it from flying away. Our puppy, Jane told us, had no interest in the pigeon. She only wanted to play with the string. *Good,* I thought. We weren't going to hunt with her anyway. We worked 9–5 jobs in Washington, DC and spent our free time training for races and exploring new restaurants. We weren't hunters.

Hunting ran in my family, though. My paternal grandfather had raised Beagles and Pointers and competed in field trials with them. My uncle Richard often hunted with his Brittanies. Growing up, my sister and I found it amusing when my parents purchased duck calls and other hunting gear for him at Christmas. Visiting their house during the holidays, we laughed at the multiple deer heads proudly displayed on their living room wall. We didn't think hunting was cool. We had never been hunting, and it seemed like an odd, old-fashioned hobby to us.

I was also, to be honest, scared of guns. In 2013, it seemed like school and other mass shootings were happening regularly. I had zero interest in owning or even touching a gun. It seemed morally wrong to be in support of guns, given the violence they could cause. So hunting with a dog or being involved in a sport where guns were used was out of the question for me. I was glad that Zara didn't seem to be interested in hunting, either.

Looking back, this was a naïve thought. We were getting a hunting dog—a dog whose ancestors had been bred for centuries to hunt game and have the instincts to point and retrieve. Not all Vizsla breeders focus on hunting competitions, however. Some are more focused on the sports of conformation, agility, and obedience. Therefore, their dogs may not have hunting instincts that are as strong as dogs from breeders who select for field ability. But that was not the case for Zara. Both of her parents had hunting titles, and so did her grandparents and great-grandparents. Little did I know where Zara and I would end up in a few short years.

Chapter 4

Building the Foundation

We drove back to Arlington with Zara in tow the night of December 11th. She rode in a crate in the car and screamed almost the whole ride home. I wasn't surprised, knowing that this was her first time away from her mother and littermates. When we arrived home, it was already getting late, but luckily Zara was tired from all the excitement. She went right into her new crate and slept almost the whole night in our bedroom. In contrast, I felt like I barely slept at all. I was on edge, listening intently in case Zara needed to go out and pee. Around 6am, I finally got up.

One of my first to-do items was to give Zara a bath. She was not thrilled about it, especially since it was winter, but she tolerated it. I tried to use my hairdryer to dry her, but she was afraid of the noise, and I didn't want to push it. As a puppy, Zara was slow to warm up to a lot of things. She was scared of loud noises and would shake when a bus or trash truck drove down the street. With a lot of encouragement, she gradually overcame these fears and would develop into a confident dog. After all the research I had done prior to getting Zara, I knew that socialization (the practice of safely exposing a puppy to a variety of new people, animals, noises, surfaces, smells, and experiences) was very important. This was my main focus for the next several months, as well as house training and general obedience.

I was with Zara almost full-time for the next three weeks. At times it was exhausting. With Christmas coming up, I was trying to get ready for the holiday, but it was difficult with an eight-week-old puppy around who would try to gnaw at any kind of decoration or present I brought out. I would wait until she fell asleep and then carefully tiptoe away, intent on making a wreath or wrapping some presents. One weekend,

Chris went to New York City to visit some friends and left me alone with Zara. After entertaining her all day that Saturday, I needed a break. I put her in her crate and drove to Georgetown in DC to walk around for two hours. I just needed to get out of the house and be alone. I was not used to spending 24/7 with another creature, and it was wearing on me.

Even though she was tiring at times, Zara was an adorable puppy, and I was smitten with her from the beginning. Chris, on the other hand, took a while to really love her. This was understandable, given that she was a ball of energy and teeth the first couple of months. Even though Chris had been the original impetus behind getting a dog, it had been a long, long time since he had had one, and he had not done nearly as much reading and research about puppies as I had.

Zara attracted a lot of attention from strangers. The first weekend we had her, Chris and I took her on a walk in our neighborhood. People driving by stopped their cars just to inquire about our cute puppy. Everyone wanted to pet her. Sometimes, it was a bit overwhelming. Owning a Vizsla is different than owning a Golden Retriever or a German Shepherd. Everyone knows those breeds, and you see them all the time. People who came up to us usually fell into two camps. Most of them had never heard of a Vizsla and were fascinated to meet this uncommon breed. But the others who did knew exactly what a Vizsla was and either owned one themselves, or had had one in the past. Vizsla owners seem to feel the need to connect with other Vizsla owners. It's almost like you are part of a special club by having one. Later on, I would find myself guilty of this, too.

By the time I had to go back to work on December 30th, Zara was almost fully house-trained and was already learning the basics of sit, lay down, and come. I could tell she was smart and picked up on things quickly. We had signed her up for a puppy kindergarten class that covered some general obedience and gave the puppies a chance to play with each other and socialize. The training facility also held a free, one-hour session on Saturday mornings called Puppy Party. They allowed puppies up to 16 weeks who'd had their initial vaccinations to come and play. We went several times, and it was as adorable as it sounds. Picture a room full of 20 puppies, all romping and playing with each other. The small breeds were separated from the larger breeds, and the training facility staff were watching the interactions and breaking things up if any of the puppies started getting too rough. Zara would come home exhausted from these sessions, and I felt like they really set the foundation for her learning proper canine behavior.

Thankfully, Chris was able to work from home the first week that I started my new job. Since we knew that he would have to go into his office the following week, we hired a dog walker. Mark was an experienced dog professional, and I felt confident leaving our new puppy in his care. He would visit twice a day for the first several weeks, letting her out to pee and feeding her lunch.

Chris worked from home two or three days a week when Zara was really young, and after a few months at my new job, my boss allowed me to work at home every Wednesday. Because of this, she was home alone only two days a week on average. Still, it was hard for me to be at work and think of my sweet puppy all alone in her crate. I knew that she had a lot of energy, and it pained me to think that she was stuck in her crate for so many hours. The only solution was to try not to think about it too much.

Her energy level was definitely difficult to manage the first few months. When I got home from work, it would already be dark. At the time, we lived in a small townhouse with only a tiny fenced patio. We would walk her around the neighborhood, but it was the middle of winter, and Zara did not like walking in the cold. At that point, we hadn't realized how essential dog coats are to Vizslas. I often felt like I didn't know what to do to entertain her all night. We would sit on the floor and play with her toys for hours. She'd run around, play tug, and retrieve toys. It almost seemed like my initial hesitations about getting a Vizsla had been correct. How was I going to deal with this dog for the next 12 to 14 years?

Thankfully, by mid-February, she'd had all of her shots and could go to the dog park in our neighborhood. Since we didn't have a yard, this was the next best thing. Although I feel differently about dog parks now, at the time, I viewed the dog park as a sanctuary. We were lucky to have this park so close. It took about 10 minutes to walk there, or two to three minutes to drive. The Fairlington dog park was about a quarter acre in size and had a crushed gravel surface. There was a large covered pavilion in the middle with a few picnic tables and a water fountain for humans and dogs. The park usually had a bunch of tennis balls and Frisbees scattered around.

The first few times we took Zara to the dog park, we went during off-hours to allow her to get used to it. At those times, only a few other dogs were there. But soon enough, I became a regular during both the morning and after-work peak times. Because of this, I got to know the people and dogs who came to the park every day. The morning group was a small cluster of retirees, whose dogs spent more time standing around than playing. The afternoon group was younger, and most of the dogs had more energy. When Zara was a puppy, it didn't matter to her. She would play with any dog that would play with her. She loved to run and chase, especially with a ball in her mouth.

Occasionally, when working at home, I would take Zara to the dog park during my lunch break. This meant that sometimes we were going there three times in one day. If I mentioned this to people at the dog park, they would look at me like I had two heads. But running her around the dog park was the easiest way to tire her out, so I had no regrets.

After Zara completed puppy kindergarten, we signed her up for a puppy obedience class at the same training facility. This class was heavy on positive reinforcement and taught us how to use clickers to train our dogs. I had never used a clicker before but found it to be a useful tool. The clicker is a small handheld device that makes a snapping sound when the metal piece is pressed. It's a consistent cue used to mark a behavior and tells the dog that a reward is coming. For example, if you ask a dog to sit, you would click the instant her butt touches the ground. Then you would give her a treat. The clicker is more precise than using your voice. Zara responded well to the clicker and was food-motivated, which made training easy. She quickly learned sit, down, and stay, and fun tricks like shake, high five, and speak.

Teaching her to walk on a loose leash was a different story. Neither Chris nor I had ever trained a dog to walk on a leash, and it proved harder than we anticipated with an energetic Vizsla puppy. In retrospect, I should have started when we first brought her home and rewarded her for walking next to me. Instead, we let her pull on the leash and just held it back, occasionally telling her "no." This was easy enough when she was

20 pounds. Once she grew into the 40-pound range, it became much more difficult. We resorted to a series of "no-pull" harnesses to slow her down. As it turned out, it would take me years until I was able to properly train her to walk on a leash. But until she was about three years old, we did not spend a lot of time taking her on long leashed walks for exercise. It didn't seem to have much effect on her energy level, so we just accepted her bad leash manners.

After meeting several of them at the temperament testing, we kept in touch with the owners of Zara's littermates. One couple, Brooke and Phill, lived about a half-hour away from us in Bethesda, Maryland. They had Zara's sister, Lily. Throughout 2014, we met up with them often for playdates. It was fun to watch Zara and Lily play together. Since they were littermates, their energy was evenly matched, and they had a great time together. I felt like I didn't have to watch them as closely as I did when Zara played with other dogs. In those instances, I was always hovering vigilantly, making sure that the other dog was not going to hurt my puppy. Seeing her play so well with Lily made me eager to seek out other Vizsla playmates, although it took a while before I was able to find any.

By the summer of 2014, Zara was developing into a lovely dog. She was sweet, extremely friendly with other people and dogs, and listened well. She loved to hang out on the couch with us and have her belly rubbed. She would perch on the back of it and watch out the window, looking very much like a princess on a throne. One of the things we worked on during the puppy obedience class was recall. The training facility we went to had a unique way of teaching recall. They advised using a word that had no meaning to the dog, since "come" or "here" was likely already something we had been using and had not always been enforcing. They recommended using the word "party" because, according to the instructor, "Who doesn't love a party?!" To condition the word, they had us spend a little time each day saying "party!" and dropping a whole bunch of high-value treats in front of our dog. Gradually, we would have our dogs at further and further distances from us before we would say the word "party." Since Zara was so food-motivated, this worked really well. As soon as we said "party," she would come running! We spent a lot of time working on this and practiced it in distracting environments, such as outside around squirrels.

Before owning a Vizsla, I had never considered that it would be necessary or useful to have a dog reliably trained with an off-leash recall. We did not realize how much off-leash exercise and running Zara would need before we got her. Even though we had read about the history of Vizslas and how they were bred to run great distances while hunting, it was not something we truly understood. When she was young, the various dog parks in the area were sufficient. But over time, having her off-leash outside of a dog park or our fenced yard became a regular occurrence.

The very first time we had Zara off-leash in an unfenced area was at a winery in Virginia wine country. This particular winery had a humongous field where visitors could sit and picnic, bordered by trees and a stream. The winery was dog-friendly and told us that dogs were allowed to run around the field as long as they were well-behaved. We visited with some friends over Memorial Day weekend in 2014, when Zara was about seven months old. After purchasing a few bottles of wine and getting set up at one of the picnic tables, some of our friends decided to kick a soccer ball around. I had Zara on her leash, but she was getting really excited about the ball and wanted to join the game. I had known that letting Zara run around the field was an option ahead of time, so I had brought pieces of cut-up hot dog, which she loved, in order to enforce her recall.

Nervously, I unclipped the leash. Zara ran around, sniffing things, obviously happy to be free. I tried out "party" a few times to make sure she would still come back to me. She obliged. She quickly joined our friends' soccer game, running exuberantly after the ball. She was having a blast. We were at the winery for a few hours on that beautiful late spring day, and Zara proved that we could trust her off-leash.

In July, I drove to visit my sister in Maryland. She lived about an hour away from us. She had recently discovered a nice hiking trail near her house, and we planned to take Zara hiking. I had started hiking with Zara when she was about four months old, and I loved how it tired her out much more than a walk in our neighborhood. She had always been leashed, though. The trail we chose ran along a river. It was very straight, and you could see far down the path. My sister had been there several times and had hardly seen anyone. After walking for a while, I decided to let Zara off-leash. I had high-value treats with me, and the trail seemed safe enough, given that there was the river on one side and a large hill on the other. As soon as I released her, she started zooming around, leaping over the high grass and bounding down the trail. She would run ahead of us and then come flying back, bouncing a few times in front us as if to say, "Let's go! You're slow!" It was adorable. This was not something I had taught her, but she seemed to naturally want to "check in" with me.

Her excitement was contagious, and I felt exhilarated watching her. The sensation stayed with me for days afterwards, and I thought about how I needed to let her experience the joy of being off-leash in the woods again. After doing some research, I discovered that there were very, very few places in the area where it was legal to have your dog off-leash. Until then, I had not realized that was the case. After all, I had had no reason to have a dog off-leash. But at this point, I realized that it was something that Zara needed. Searching out places where she could safely be off-leash would become somewhat of an obsession over the next few years.

We continued to hike with Zara over that summer, and we still went to the dog park a lot. She was growing up, and at the end of August, she had her first heat cycle at 10.5 months old. Neither Chris nor I had ever experienced a dog in heat before, but we had prepared for this moment. Our breeder had instructed us to buy fabric dog panties and put pads or pantyliners intended for human menstruation inside them. Her heat cycle wasn't really a big deal. She wore the panties inside the house, but we took them off when she was in her crate or outside. The hardest part was not being able to go to the dog park or have her off-leash. When female dogs are in heat, they smell very attractive to males, and the last thing we wanted was for Zara to become pregnant. Thankfully, we had moved over the summer to a house with a small fenced yard, so we were able to play ball and other games outside with her. Our neighbors across the street also had a fenced yard for their two Bassett Hounds. They were neutered, so Zara was able to visit with them during her cycle.

Her heat cycle lasted about 24 days, slightly longer than the usual 21 days. I was thrilled when we finally could take her back to the dog park. I could tell she missed her dog friends because she was so excited to see them. Unfortunately, our return was short-lived. That same week, she got bitten by a dog in our neighborhood and had to spend more time recovering.

There was a guy who lived several houses down from us with a middle-aged female Boxer. This neighbor was very friendly and suggested that our dogs play together. At the time, Zara would play with any dog who was willing, so I figured it was fine. One day, he came by our house and asked if he could see if his dog wanted to play with Zara. "Okay," I said, and opened the gate to our fence. The Boxer stood in the threshold, looking at Zara, but not moving. She didn't seem inclined to enter the yard, so the guy shrugged and walked on.

The next time I saw him was a few weeks later, as it was getting dark one evening. Again, he asked if his dog could play with Zara. We were outside in our yard. I obliged and opened the gate. This time, the Boxer came in. She stood in our yard for a few minutes. Zara circled around her, obviously interested in her new visitor. The next thing I knew, the Boxer had pinned Zara to the ground and was biting her head. I was terrified. I don't know how we managed to get them apart, but thankfully the Boxer released her hold on Zara and her owner started apologizing profusely. I could tell Zara had a bite mark above her eye, but it didn't look too bad. I took her inside to show Chris, and he was furious that I had let the Boxer into our yard. What I didn't know was that our neighbor had tried to get the boxer to play with Zara a third time, when Chris was home, but the Boxer had growled at Zara. The guy neglected to tell me that.

Chris examined the bite mark and decided that we needed to get to the emergency vet right away. As we left, our neighbor told us that he would pay for Zara's vet bills. We drove to the closest vet at nine o'clock that night. Thankfully, they were able to see Zara quickly and checked her eye for damage. The vet said that the dog's tooth had come very close to piercing her cornea, but thankfully it had not. She shaved the area around the bite mark and cleaned it out. She returned Zara to us, drugged up and wearing a plastic cone around her neck. I scooped her up and hugged her tight, sobbing. I couldn't believe that I had been the one to cause my baby injury. I was so grateful that she wouldn't have permanent damage from the bite.

Afterward, we found out from our neighbors across the street that the guy's Boxer had bitten other dogs in the neighborhood. Chris and I were appalled. He had tricked us, making us think that his dog was friendly, when he knew otherwise. Thankfully, he did pay for Zara's vet bills, but we avoided him after that.

I was relieved to find that Zara did not seem to suffer any emotional damage from the bite. Sometimes when incidents like this happen, a dog can become afraid or aggressive toward other dogs. But that was not the case. For a while, it seemed as though Zara avoided other Boxers, but maybe that was just me projecting my feelings onto her. It took me a long time before I didn't tense up when I saw one at the dog park.

On October 11, 2014, Zara turned one year old. This felt like a milestone. We had managed to raise a Vizsla puppy through the first year. Although Zara was a wonderful dog, it was still a lot of work. To celebrate, I wanted to throw Zara a party for her first birthday. I spoke with her littermate's owner, Brooke, and we decided to host a joint party for Zara and Lily. We held the party at Brooke's house and invited our families and several dog friends. We made cupcakes that were safe for dogs and gave out Frisbees as party favors. Several years prior, my coworker had held a birthday party for her dog. I attended at the time, feeling a bit silly. *A birthday party for a dog?*

The times had changed, though, and now I was doing the same thing. It didn't bother me in the least. I was a dog mom now, and I had no problem embracing the label.

Chapter 5

Trying Something New

Shortly after Zara's first birthday, her breeder reached out to see if I was interested in entering Zara in an upcoming AKC Junior Hunting Test. The local Vizsla club, the Conestoga Vizsla Club, would be holding a hunting test in December. Jane told me that the junior level was mostly natural ability, and it was a low-pressure event. It did not involve shooting birds. Although hunting was not something I was particularly interested in, if it involved Zara, I was willing to try. Even though Zara had not shown a strong hunting desire during the temperament testing, she had become very interested in squirrels and chipmunks that fall. Every time we let her outside, she would slowly stalk out the door, looking for potential victims. She had killed one squirrel and captured two chipmunks, although we had gotten those away from her while they were still alive. Zara had never seen live game birds before, so Jane suggested that we meet at a local wildlife management area (WMA) to expose her to some quail. Those were the birds that would be used in the hunting test.

The WMA had a designated dog training area with several fields of long grasses. I was as excited to let Zara run off-leash as I was for her to find birds. Jane brought Zara's mother, Caiya, and her littermate Max along. Jane had kept Zara's other brother Benny from the litter, but Benny was away with his professional trainer learning to be a bird dog. Jane was hoping to run him in field trials when he was older.

Jane also brought several live quail with her, and we planted one in the field under a small wire foot trap to make sure it wouldn't move. After it was planted, we released Zara to see if she could locate the quail. She found it pretty quickly but was a little afraid of it at first. She jumped back when it moved and then crept up towards it again. Ideally, when a pointing dog, such as a Vizsla, smells a bird, they should freeze and stand in a rigid stance known as a point. This indicates to the owner where the bird is located. She kind of pointed at it, but her tail wagged instead of being motionless. We stroked her tail to get it to stop and remain straight. Then Jane released the bird from the trap and it flew away. Zara didn't have much interest in chasing it.

After that sequence, we brought Caiya out to see if Zara would follow her around and learn from her. Caiya took off sprinting, totally focused on hunting. She had her Junior Hunter title and had been in several field trials, so she knew the game. Zara followed her, but I don't think she was completely sure what she was supposed to be doing yet.

After that run, I put Zara in my car to give her a break, and we got Max out. Max also seemed ready to hunt birds, and he wasn't afraid. He pointed the first bird right away. Max and Caiya ran around some more, and when Max came upon the next bird, he *really* wanted it and tried to catch it before Jane could step in to kick it up. Jane said he definitely got Caiya's hunting desire.

Finally, we got Zara out again, and she seemed to get the hang of it after a couple more repetitions. She still seemed a little scared of the birds but was getting more excited about finding them. Jane said she remembered from the temperament testing that Zara was a little slow to warm up to things and had to learn at her own pace.

Afterwards, she slept the whole way home and stayed on the couch the whole evening as well. It was fun to see her try something new, and it seemed like she did have some desire to hunt birds, after all.

Since then, I've talked to people who say that the first time they saw their dog point a bird was a life-changing moment for them. Even if they were not interested in bird hunting before, they were amazed by their dog's abilities and couldn't wait to dive into training. That was not the case for me. Even though I enjoyed the outing, in my mind, nothing spectacular had happened. I was willing to pursue it further, but this was not the moment I got hooked.

I sent in my registration form for the hunting test in December but found out that it had already filled up. Jane told me that the Conestoga Vizsla Club would host another test in the spring, likely in March. I was fine with this. Zara and I had plenty of other things to keep us occupied.

Since Zara had turned a year old in October, Chris and I had started running with her. We had waited until this time to make sure we didn't do any damage to her growth plates. It had been hard waiting 10 months, but we didn't want to impact her long-term health. When the time came, it was exciting to actually be able to run with her, since that was one of the main reasons we had wanted a Vizsla in the first place. We gradually increased her mileage until she was running three miles twice a week with us.

Zara turned out to be a fantastic running partner. We never spent much time training her how to run with us. She seemed to naturally understand it. She didn't try to stop and sniff when we were running. Once we started, it was like she entered a work mode and would go for as long as we wanted. Of course, she pulled the whole time. We probably should have spent the time when she was younger teaching her not to do this, but, honestly, we didn't really know how. So instead, we were pulled along, which certainly helped on hills!

I eventually came to realize that Chris and I would never be able to run enough for Zara. Maybe we could have if we were marathon or ultra-marathon runners who ran many miles every single day of the week. But we weren't. On average, we'd run two to three times a week for 3–6 miles, and that was it. *Runner's World* magazine certainly was right about Vizslas being able to go faster than a seven-minute mile pace. Zara did not appreciate my slower eight- and nine-minute mile paces. Eventually, she would become so fit that even three miles at a fast clip wouldn't tire her out much. We'd come back and she'd give us an expectant look like, "That was fun. What's next?!"

I had also started to connect with other local Vizsla owners and meet up with them for playdates and hikes. Over the previous year, I regularly posted photos of Zara's antics to her Instagram account. Through this platform, I met several other young women who owned Vizslas in the area.

By early 2015, I had started meeting frequently with Elizabeth, who owned Lily; Alex, who owned Archer and Gatsby; and Jessica, who owned Piper. All of the Vizslas were young and energetic like Zara. We'd take them to deserted hiking areas and let them run loose. They had a blast. Elizabeth, Alex, Jessica, and I would walk along and talk about everything related to our dogs. I loved these adventures, and I'd go home with a tired Vizsla.

In January of that year, Chris and I decided to start sending Zara to daycare once a week. We were both still working outside of our home most of the time, and we felt that having a dog walker visit during the day really didn't do anything for her energy level. She'd still be crazy in the evenings. I was hesitant to send her to a typical dog daycare that was held in a large indoor room. I didn't want her to have to pee inside, and I wasn't sure that she would love a huge group of dogs, since she sometimes became overwhelmed when we went to a large dog park. Fortunately, the previous summer, we had bumped into a guy while hiking who ran a Vizsla-only daycare called Vizsland. Yes, there were enough Vizslas in the DC area to make this feasible. His name was Chad, and he lived in northwest DC in a large house with a yard. He was inspired to start Vizsland because of his own Vizsla, Gatsby. He'd have up to 10 Vizslas at his house each day, and they would play in his yard, hang out inside on his couches, and once a day, he'd take them hiking off-leash in the nearby park. It sounded like heaven.

Zara was still intact at this point, and we were not planning on spaying her yet. Chad was willing to accommodate that, which Chris and I really appreciated, given that most daycares require dogs to be spayed or neutered at six months. Zara was already 15 months old. He had one intact male who also attended daycare, so Chad would let us know when he would be there, and we would pick a different day, just to be safe. We took Zara to do a meet-and-greet at his house during the Martin Luther King Jr. holiday weekend, and she did great. Chris and I were excited to send her to Vizsland the following week.

The only unfortunate part of taking her to Vizsland was its location. We lived in Alexandria, Virginia, and Chad lived in upper northwest DC, which was about 11 miles from us. Without any traffic, it would only take about 25 minutes to get there. But given that we were traveling to and from Vizsland during rush hour, it took significantly longer. On days when Zara went to Vizsland, I would leave our house at 7:15 am. It would usually take about 45 minutes to get there with all the traffic.

I'd drop her off around 8, and then head to my office in downtown DC. By the time I'd get to my office, it would be 8:40, or 8:30, if I was lucky. In the evenings, I'd stay at my office a little later and leave to pick her up around 6pm. It would take about 20 minutes to get to Vizsland. By the time I had thanked Chad and gotten her in the car, I could get onto Rock Creek Parkway to get back to Virginia. Before 6:30pm on weekdays, all the lanes of Rock Creek Parkway were one way going north, so I had to wait until after the lanes switched back to take it. We'd usually get home around 7pm.

I was spending about two-and-a-half hours in the car on the days that Zara went to Vizsland, but I didn't mind. I felt much better when I was at work on those days, knowing she was not alone at home and she was being properly exercised.

In February, I met up with Zara's breeder, Jane, again at the same wildlife management area we'd been to the previous fall. The Conestoga Vizsla Club was holding another hunting test in March, and I'd submitted my application early this time, intent on getting in. Jane brought Zara's mother Caiya and her brother Benny, who was back from his trainer. I also invited my friend Alex and her boyfriend Pablo to come with her Vizsla, Archer. She was interested in entering the test, too.

Zara and I were the first to arrive, and I let her run around the field for a little while to burn off some energy. I think she remembered being at the training area and started leaping around right away. When Archer arrived with his owners, the two of them began running like crazy, chasing each other and exploring all the wonders that the field held—lots of various poops, patches of ice, a jaw bone from an unidentified animal, and a fresh skull of a dead animal, maybe a fox. I had a very difficult time getting the skull away from Zara until Pablo and I offered her treats. At 16 months, obedience was still a work-in-progress in highly stimulating environments.

When Jane arrived, she set out two quail under small foot traps so they couldn't fly away immediately. We took Caiya, Zara, and Archer out. Caiya was all business, nose to the ground, and Zara and Archer followed after her, not wanting to miss out. Caiya pointed the first bird, and soon Zara and Archer came upon it as well. Both of the youngsters were a bit timid around the bird at first and not quite sure whether to point or pounce on it. Archer wanted to do more pouncing than Zara. Zara still seemed timid, but I tried not to baby her too much and just encouraged her to keep moving after Jane released the bird.

The dogs found the second caged bird soon after, and Zara did point that one more convincingly. I stroked her tail up and praised her. After the bird was released and flew off, we started heading back in the direction of the parking area. Zara was somewhat ahead of us when I saw her stop. As I approached, I could see she was pointing, with good form. She held the point for maybe 5–10 seconds, which was an improvement over her previous points. Then she moved in and the bird flew up. She seemed to be starting to understand what she should be doing. After a few more minutes, she found the bird again and pointed it a second time! It was cool to see her beginning to get it.

Then Jane put Caiya back in her car and got Benny out. He had been with his trainer for the past six months, so he looked like an old pro in the field and found the first bird almost immediately. I think Zara and Archer may have been getting a little tired at this point, because this was when Zara located the animal skull and started playing with it instead of hunting.

I enjoyed watching the Vizslas doing what they were bred to do. I also liked the aftermath. Zara was out in the field for about three hours that day, running for most of the time, and she slept on the couch the rest of the evening after we got home. Figuring out how to tire out my young Vizsla was a daily priority. I savored the occasions when she was truly exhausted from a fun day of activities.

Unfortunately, we did not get to participate in the hunting test that spring, either. The weekend it was supposed to be held ended up being very snowy and icy, and the test was canceled. I was disappointed but figured we could try again in the fall.

For the rest of that spring and summer, we continued to do the other activities we enjoyed with Zara. We ran, went hiking, and took her to dog-friendly places. I tried twice to earn an AKC Canine Good Citizen (CGC) title with her, but we failed both times. The CGC test evaluates the dog on basic obedience, its ability to interact with strangers and be calm around other dogs. The last part of that test is a "supervised separation" where the owner goes out of sight for three minutes and the dog stays with the person running the test. Both times, this proved to be too much for my Velcro dog. She'd be fine for a minute or two, but then started yelping for me, which is not allowed.

Chris and I had gotten engaged the previous summer, and our wedding was set for early October in 2015. Zara, of course, would be in our wedding. We planned to have her walk/run down the aisle during the ceremony. I wanted her to carry a basket of flowers and I spent several months trying to teach her to do so. This was my first foray into any sort of retrieve training, and it was difficult. I never thought to watch videos on retrieve training for bird dogs, but that probably would have made it a lot easier. Even though Zara loved to retrieve her toys, she didn't like putting strange objects in her mouth. I attributed this to the way we raised her as a puppy—any time she picked up something she wasn't supposed to have, we scolded her to drop it. Because of this, she had developed a very clear idea of what was hers and what was not, but that did not help in the retrieving department. This would continue to be an issue for me several years down the road, when I attempted to teach her how to retrieve birds.

Eventually, Zara learned to take the basket from me and carry it, but I didn't spend enough time proofing the behavior in high-distraction environments. The day of our wedding, she had no interest in taking the basket when we tried to practice before the ceremony. There was just too much going on. Instead, she ended up running down the aisle without it. The DJ played the song "Who Let the Dogs Out?" and we used her "party" recall command, yelling, "Zara, PARTY!" The guests loved it.

Chapter 6

The Lightbulb Moment

Once again, in November 2015, the Conestoga Vizsla Club's fall hunting test was approaching. I reached out to Jane to see if she could meet up to expose Zara to birds one more time before the test. Since it had been nine months since she'd seen a quail, I wasn't sure she'd remember what to do. Instead, Jane suggested that we enter a local walking field trial that had a special category called a Hunting Dog Stake. This would give us a taste of being at an actual event. The American Kennel Club's Field Trials for pointing dogs generally consist of four main entry categories. The Puppy Stake is for puppies under 15 months. The Derby Stake is for dogs under two years. In these two stakes, the judges are looking at the dogs' hunting ability, and further, in Derby, the ability to find birds and point. However, they don't have to have much training beyond that.

The remaining categories are for "finished" dogs: an Amateur Gun Dog Stake is for any dog with a handler who is not a professional trainer and an Open Gun Dog Stake allows both amateurs and professionals. The Hunting Dog Stake was for dogs of any age who had not placed in any trials. There were no age limits. At that point, Zara had just turned two, so she was too old for the Derby Stake but definitely not ready for Gun Dog Stakes. The Hunting Dog Stake seemed perfect. It was being judged with the same rules as Derby.

The field trial was held on a freezing cold Sunday in mid-November. Zara and I arrived early to the grounds, which were located on a private farm in southern Maryland. Jane also came to the field trial with Zara's mother, Caiya. She had entered Caiya in the Amateur Gun Dog Stake. We had to wait a while for Zara to run, which she was not happy about.

When it was finally Zara's time to compete, she was super excited. She was paired with another dog, a Brittany. The other handler and I walked into the field with the judges riding behind us in an all-terrain vehicle (ATV). After we let the dogs go, Zara took off. It had been a long time since we had done any bird training, and I wasn't sure if she'd remember what to do. As I walked the first half of the course, she was just running around like she normally did when we went hiking. Finally, she found a bird.

She pointed the bird, and I called out to the judges to let them know. Then I was supposed to kick up ("flush") the bird to get it to fly and shoot a blank pistol, which I had borrowed from Jane. In bird dog training and trials, a small pistol with the end plugged is used with blank ammunition to imitate the noise of a gun if a bird isn't being shot. I tried kicking around the bird but it wouldn't fly! It looked kind of sad and was rolling around in the grass. Zara broke her point and tried to play with it. One of the judges told me to just kick it and shoot the gun. I tried to get the gun to fire but I wasn't able to pull the trigger hard enough. I just didn't have the finger strength to do it. The judge looked at me like I was an idiot. He got up from the ATV, took the gun from me, and fired it. I thanked him, feeling embarrassed. I think a different quail flew up then. It must have been near the one that Zara was pointing. As soon as Zara saw the bird fly, it was like a light bulb went off in her head. She was like, "That is what I am supposed to be looking for!" She ran after it as it headed into a tree. Then she took off in the field, sniffing away. She was flying along. She didn't find any more birds in the last part of the course, because I think most of the birds had been planted in the first part of the field we walked through.

When the judges indicated our time was up, I blew my whistle to get Zara to come, and she bounded right to me. Per Jane's recommendation, I had recently bought a whistle to use during field events like this one. Zara was listening to me really well that day, which made me happy. I could tell she didn't want to stop hunting. In fact, after she was finished, Jane and I were standing off of the course for a while with Zara on a leash and she was crying to go out into the field again.

After all the dogs were finished, one of the club members announced the placements. Zara got fourth place and a ribbon! There were six dogs total in the Hunting Dog Stake. It was exciting to hear her name called, even though I didn't know if the other two dogs had done poorly. I really had no idea of the criteria she was being judged on, and, to be honest, I didn't care. I was just happy that she'd had fun. Although she'd been somewhat scared of the quail a year ago, her interest seemed to be increasing each time that she encountered birds.

After the field trial, I was looking forward to the hunting test in early December. Our entry was confirmed, the weather was supposed to be good, and a year after we had tried to get involved, it was finally going to happen. The test was held about an hour and 20 minutes from my house, at the site where we'd first met Zara's mother over two years ago. I arrived early, and we had to wait a couple of hours until it was her turn to run. Zara, of course, was getting very impatient during this time. Our friends Alex and Pablo were there with Archer, as well.

During hunting tests, dogs are braced together in groups of two. For her brace, Zara was paired with a seven-year-old Vizsla named Gracie, who already had her Junior Hunter title. She was competing to earn her Junior Hunter Advanced title, which I didn't know existed. Her owner explained to me that after they earn the JH title, they have to get 5 more passes, using the same criteria that they are judged on for Junior Hunter, but they have to earn an average of 8 in all four categories. The categories are hunting, bird finding ability, pointing, and trainability. I wasn't aware there was a 0–10 scale for judging. I found out later that the dogs have to get a minimum of 5 in all categories and at least an average of 7 to pass. There were so many new things to learn. I had come to this event with no expectations and minimal knowledge—just thinking of it as something fun to do with my dog. Looking back, this sense of zero expectation was a nice place to be. Never again would I feel such a low level of pressure going into a hunting event. I truly would have been okay with any outcome that day. If Zara had not done well at the test, we would have moved on to something else.

After what seemed like forever, the judges were ready for us, and it was Zara and Gracie's turn to run. Both of the judges were on horseback, and Zara was a little scared of the horses at first. She actually barked at them. She had met a horse before, but it had been a while. I encouraged her to get in front of them and once she started running, she didn't care about them anymore.

The course was a big field with areas of waist-high brush interspersed with areas that had been cut down. Zara took off and after a few minutes, found a bird! She pointed it, and I attempted to shoot the blank pistol but again had trouble. I couldn't believe I was embarrassing myself for the second time. Thankfully, the other handler shot his for me. Once the bird flew, Zara and Gracie chased it over a little hill. They were cutting the course, and the other handler and I called them to try to get them back on track. They weren't coming back, so the judges rode through the brush on their horses to see where they went. They crested the hill and paused. "Hurry up!" they called. "Both dogs are on point!"

The other guy and I tramped over there as quickly as we could. I saw Zara and Gracie both pointing the same bird. The judges called it a "divided find" and commented how beautiful they looked. We both fired our guns (I actually got mine to fire!), and Zara and Gracie took off again.

Both dogs found a third bird after a few minutes and then a fourth one at the very end of the course in the woods. It was cool because they were finding the birds together like they were used to hunting with each other.

Zara was hot and tired at the end of her run, but she did look satisfied. When we got the score sheet back, I saw that we had gotten 10/10 on everything! I felt really happy and proud of Zara, especially since she hadn't had much formal bird training and a lot of it was clearly her natural instinct. However, I could take some credit for the trainability aspect, because it had to do with how well she listened to me and followed my commands. I had spent a lot of time with Zara off-leash in the woods or in fields and she was used to being in front of me but also checking in and getting directional signals from me. It was nice to see that all my time doing that had paid off.

On Sunday, there was a smaller group of handlers and dogs at the hunting test, and we were not there as long. Zara had a good run again, although she only found two birds, and I felt like she was a little more tired and didn't run quite as hard as Saturday. Her bracemate this time was a three-year-old male Vizsla named Jack, but he seemed more interested in humping her than finding birds. After we let them go, Zara took off, and Jack went after her, trying to have some fun. Zara took a running snap at him, as if to say, "Leave me alone! I've got birds to find!"

We also earned perfect 10 scores on Sunday and another Junior Hunter pass. After we finished, one of the judges asked me who Zara's breeder was and I gave her Jane's name. Later that night, the Facebook messages started flowing in. Jane had heard that everyone was talking about this young female Vizsla and how well she did at the test. I got a message from Laura Miller, who owned Zara's sire, Bull, and lived in Iowa at the time. One of the judges from Saturday was friends with Laura and had called to tell her how impressed he was with Zara's performance. The last time he gave out perfect 10 scores when judging, he said, was five years ago.

I was flattered. It was almost hard to believe how well she did. Zara had transformed from a puppy with no bird desire into a bird hunting machine with hardly any work from me. I guess I shouldn't have been surprised. It seemed like every time I looked on Facebook, Laura was posting about another one of Bull's field trial wins. He wasn't just winning local trials, either. He was winning national competitions against dozens of other dogs. That year, he had won the National Gun Dog Championship, a countrywide walking field trial put on by the Vizsla Club of America. At seven years old, he was first amongst 44 other Vizslas. Bull almost seemed to possess a star quality, and it looked like Zara had inherited some of that, too.

Even though I was out of my element, I really enjoyed the hunting test, and I was starting to see how this sort of thing could become addicting. It was so cool to see Zara doing what she was bred to do, and she clearly loved it. After that weekend, she had two passes toward her Junior Hunter title and only needed two more. I planned to enter her in a spring hunting test, and I hoped to finish her title then. She needed four passes total to become a Junior Hunter.

At the beginning of 2016, I finally decided to buy an electronic collar (e-collar) for Zara. Up until that point, when I had Zara off-leash, I simply relied on her training and cooperation to recall her back to me. Most of the time, this worked fine. She had a natural tendency to check in with me on hikes, which was something I never taught her. However, after a few scares, I decided that we needed an e-collar as a safety precaution. Several of the Vizsla friends that I hiked with used them with good results. One day, I was hiking a trail with Zara, my friend Jessica, and her Vizsla, Piper. Zara saw a deer and took off after it, even as I yelled at her to leave it and come back. She disappeared out of sight for what felt like hours, but was probably only a few seconds. Roads were not that far away, and I feared the worst. However, she returned not long afterwards, looking like she had no regrets.

Electronic collars are a training tool for dogs. The dog wears a collar with a receiver around their neck, and the human carries a wireless remote that delivers various levels of electrical stimulation. E-collars are useful in delivering a precise correction when the dog is at a great distance from the handler. When used properly, they don't hurt the dog and, in certain circumstances, can save a dog's life. For example, if your dog is chasing an animal and is about to run into a road with oncoming cars, an e-collar correction can snap them out of the moment faster than your voice can. Many e-collars also come with tone/beep and vibrate functions.

I did some research and decided on a Garmin brand e-collar with the ability to use tone, vibrate, and 18 levels of stimulation. It had a three-quarters of a mile range and a bark collar function as well. Zara spent a little too much time in our yard barking up trees at squirrels, so I thought I might want to use that feature. It also had the ability to add two more dogs to the remote, in case we decided to get another dog in the future.

I watched several videos on how to train your dog to an e-collar and wanted to try doing it myself. The first thing you were supposed to do was figure out your dog's lowest "working level." The videos advised to use the "momentary" stimulation button, starting on the lowest level 1. I was supposed to press the button for a second and watch for any sort of indication from Zara that she felt it. The videos said that she would give a slight turn of the head or flick of an ear. I tried level 1, and she didn't react. Level 2. No reaction. Level 3. No reaction. Finally, on level 4, she gave a slight indication that she felt it. *Great*, I thought. *Level 4 is her lowest working level.*

Unfortunately, I didn't know enough about e-collars to realize that there is a big difference between the momentary nick and the continuous stimulation. A dog might feel a nick only slightly at a high level because it's just for an instant. But they definitely will feel the continuous stimulation. Also, I probably did not have the collar on tight enough. If it's not snug, the dog may not feel the stimulation when their head is in certain positions.

I took Zara outside on a long leash. I was planning on using the e-collar to reinforce "come," a command she knew very well. Once she walked a few feet from me and was distracted, I would tug on the leash and press the continuous stimulation button as I called "come." As soon as she turned toward me to come, I would stop the stimulation on the e-collar.

Zara started sniffing the ground when we got outside. I allowed her to move away from me, and then I said "come" while pressing the continuous stimulation button on level 4. She yelped as soon as I pressed the button and came running towards me with terror in her eyes.

Oh, no, what did I do? I thought. *I thought level 4 was the correct level!*

Zara was shaking like a leaf beside me. "It's okay, baby," I said, petting her. "I'm sorry!" There was no way I could continue the training session. Every time I moved a step, Zara moved with me. She wasn't going to move far enough away to allow me to recall her. I sighed and took the collar and leash off of her, figuring I'd try again tomorrow.

Unfortunately, that one incident made Zara scared every time the e-collar came out. Instead of more training, I decided to have her wear it every time we did something fun, like a walk or a hike, so she would come to learn that the e-collar meant fun adventures. This took a while. For the next several days, I could walk her in the neighborhood with the e-collar on and she would stay glued to my side, walking perfectly. That had never happened before. I also took her hiking with two other Vizsla friends, and she hardly ranged from me at all, even though she was off-leash. It was sad, and I felt bad for causing this negative association.

Gradually, Zara became more accustomed to wearing the e-collar, and eventually, was not bothered by it. I started using the tone function to recall her and found that she responded instantly to that. Her recall was already solid, and wearing the e-collar made her listen a little better. So, for the next three years, I never used the stimulation levels with her. At that point, I would try again to use the e-collar properly and would be more successful.

In March, I entered her in another Junior Hunting Test, hoping to finish her title. She needed two more passes. We had not done any training on live birds since the last test in December, but I wasn't worried about how she would do. The Mason-Dixon German Shorthaired Pointer Club held the test at McKee-Beshers Wildlife Management Area, which was where I had met Jane the previous year to do some training. There were a few Vizslas there, but mostly German Shorthaired Pointers and other pointing breeds.

It was a double-double hunting test, so they had sessions for Junior Hunter in the morning and afternoon of the same day. The weather was cooler than the hunting test in the fall and it was also slightly rainy. But it was better for Zara that it was cool.

In her first brace, she ran early in the morning with a German Shorthaired Pointer puppy. She found several birds and ran well. In the afternoon, she was paired with a Wirehaired Pointing Griffon who was new to the hunting test world and did not pass. Again, Zara ran quite well, but about halfway through the test, she found a quail in the woods that was injured or tired and wouldn't fly. I tried to get her out of the woods, but she was not listening to me and just wanted to play with the quail. Being a new handler, I didn't really know what to do. The judges weren't offering any advice. I wasn't sure if I was allowed to grab her collar and pull her out of the woods or not. Because of that, we got docked in trainability, but her scores were still 9's and 10's. She earned two more Junior Hunter passes that day, and her AKC name became Trailside's Tzar of Fairlington JH.

It was an exciting day. I was proud of Zara, and since Chris, my parents, my sister, and our breeder Jane all came to watch, I had plenty of people for the celebration.

Chapter 7

Choose the Bigger Life

Less than a month after Zara completed her Junior Hunter title, Chris and I moved from Alexandria, Virginia to Raleigh, North Carolina. We had been discussing this move for two years and had finally made it happen. Chris was the driving force—he had lived in the DC area for 15 years and was ready for something different. He was fed up with the traffic, expensive housing, and pace of life. I had lived there for seven years and really liked the area. But I also recognized that if we wanted to buy a house, that was going to be very difficult in Northern Virginia.

We picked Raleigh after doing some research. Neither of us had family in Raleigh, nor did we have jobs pulling us there. But Raleigh was about four hours south of DC, which meant it had milder winters. It was a small city with a low cost of living, much less traffic, and it was known for being progressive, with a well-educated population. We rented a two-bedroom apartment for our first year, paying $1,000 a month; we had paid $2,000 a month in Northern Virginia for the same thing.

We moved to Raleigh on April 1, 2016. It was a bit scary starting over, without knowing anyone. However, I knew that Zara could help me meet new friends. People were always trying to say hi to her when we were out in public, and I knew that I just needed to find more crazy Vizsla people like me. This turned out to be more difficult than I anticipated, however. It seemed like Raleigh had a much smaller population of Vizslas, and there was no organized meet-up group. I did meet a few people through Instagram, but I missed the group of girls that I used to hike with in DC.

At the same time, I had quit my job and, with Chris' encouragement, decided to start my own graphic design business. I had been freelancing off and on since I got out of grad school, but building my client list took some time. My schedule was totally different than it had been when we lived in the DC area. Instead of going to an office four days a week, I now worked at home all the time. This was great for Zara—she was not alone for extended periods of time, and she loved all the togetherness. Since we now lived in an apartment, we had to be extra-vigilant to make sure she was getting enough exercise. My weekdays took on the following rhythm: wake up at 7am, take Zara out to pee on a leash, eat breakfast and feed her, get ready, and then drive to the nearby dog park around 7:45. We'd stay there for about 45 minutes, then I'd come back to the apartment and work until lunchtime. Around 12:30, I'd walk her to our apartment's dog park, which was a small, fenced space where she'd run around and chase bugs. We were typically the only people there, although I eventually got to know the other dog owners who lived in the complex.

In the afternoons, I'd walk her to get our mail around 2:30 or 3, and then we'd go to the large dog park or do something else around 5pm or so. I spent a lot of time alone and had a lot of time to think during this period. In regards to Zara's hunting activities, I felt that I had reached a decision point. While she had excelled at the Junior Hunter level, I knew that training her for the next level of competition—whether that was Senior Hunting Tests or Field Trial Gun Dog Stakes—was going to be a lot of work. At a minimum, I had to get her "steady"—where she would stay still during the flight of the bird and the resulting gunshot instead of chasing—in order to run her in AKC Field Trials. It seemed like a daunting task. Although I loved the process of training Zara, I had no access to live birds and I didn't know anyone in the Raleigh area who was training their Vizsla for hunting. It was unfortunate timing that we had moved away from DC, because if we had stayed, I could have gotten more help from Zara's breeder.

Although I had a basic idea of what I needed to do, I didn't fully comprehend everything that was involved in getting Zara to that level. I had never seen a Gun Dog Stake or an upper level hunting test in person. The main reason I wanted to do field trials was because the few people I knew who competed with their Vizslas did them. I also didn't want to have to kill birds, so field trials, with their blank guns, seemed like a good option. At that point, I didn't realize that some field trial stakes involve retrieving, too. A lot of AKC Field Trials allow horseback handling, where the handler rides a horse as the dog runs ahead. There are also walking trials, where the handler is on foot. I was definitely more interested in walking trials, because I wasn't comfortable riding a horse.

Even though I knew it would be difficult, I felt like I had to give Zara the chance. Maybe I would never own another dog like her. Chris and I had underestimated the amount of work owning a Vizsla involved, and I wasn't sure he would agree to get another Vizsla in the future. Maybe this would be my only chance to have a dog like this, especially one with such innate talent. I decided to go for it, not really understanding the road that lay ahead. I just knew that I wanted to try. One of my favorite authors, Gretchen Rubin, instructs people to "Choose the bigger life" when you're trying to make an important decision. Which option will bring more opportunities? More growth? More challenges? More love?

Deciding to train Zara for advanced bird work was certainly choosing the bigger life. I had no idea what lay in store for us, but I was ready to find out.

The question was, what now? I wasn't sure where to start, so I reached out to Jane to see if she knew anyone in the Raleigh area. She gave me a few leads, but most of the people she knew lived several hours away. I went to Facebook and posted to the large Vizsla International Facebook group, which has members from all over the world. Doing this led me to a woman named Kim, who lived in nearby Wake Forest, NC and was training her two-year-old Vizsla, Frankie, for field trials and hunt tests. She belonged to a hunt club about 40 minutes south of where I lived and invited me to visit it with her in a few weeks.

Zara and I met up with her on a warm Friday morning in early June. The hunt club had a large pond in the middle, several fields, and a pigeon coop with live pigeons. Bird dog owners often use homing pigeons to train their pointing dogs because they can be reused. Pigeons can be taught to return back to their coop. A pigeon can be placed under a small metal cage or in an electronic bird launcher, and, after the pigeon is released, it will fly off and return to its coop. The pigeons aren't harmed and can be used again and again. With all of this, the hunt club seemed like an ideal location to train your dog.

I let Zara run around in the field for a bit, and then Kim went to the pigeon coop to get some pigeons. Zara had never hunted pigeons before, but she had no trouble finding them when Kim put them out in the field. She pointed and then chased them when I flushed. I talked to Kim about my desire to have Zara compete at higher levels of bird dog competitions. I asked her if the hunt club was open to new members, and she told me that, unfortunately, they were full and weren't accepting any. I was disappointed, but figured I'd find another place to train. I thanked Kim for inviting us and headed home.

At home, on my lunch breaks, when Zara ran around our apartment dog park, I would search the internet on my phone to find places to train. I looked up bird dog breeders, hunting preserves, and public land. I searched dog trainers and hunting clubs. I contacted several. Living in the South, I had thought that it would be easy to find a place to train Zara and have access to birds. *Didn't everyone hunt down here?* Unfortunately, it didn't seem like that was the case. Everything I found was too far away for me to go on a regular basis. Many bird dog trainers take dogs as boarding clients, and they stay for several months, but I never seriously considered sending Zara away. This was supposed to be something I was doing because it was fun, and I knew being apart from Zara would not be fun.

Chapter 8

Looking for Opportunities

Shortly after we moved to Raleigh, Zara began to have digestive issues. This was not new. When Zara was a puppy, we had fed her the grain-free kibble that her breeder recommended, and she had not had any problems with it. However, when she was about 15 months old, she began to lose weight and have a lot of loose stools. I switched her to a more calorie-dense, grain-free kibble, but it didn't seem to help. After a few months of that, I decided to try a grain-inclusive kibble. We didn't really see much improvement. She had a few episodes of vomiting and diarrhea, and one night in January, we ended up at the emergency vet because she didn't seem well. We didn't get any clear answers about what was wrong with her. The vet seemed focused on treating the symptoms, not trying to find the cause.

This happened again in April, and the vet at the emergency clinic recommended putting her on a hydrolyzed protein diet, which is a special kibble that is supposed to be easier for dogs to digest because the protein is already broken down. I was skeptical. I had done a lot of research about dog nutrition up until that point, and I didn't buy the message that a highly-processed diet with questionable ingredients was really the best for my baby.

I knew that some people fed their dogs a raw meat diet. I had learned about this when I was searching the Vizsla Forum before we got Zara. People referred to it as the BARF (Bones and Raw Food or Biologically Appropriate Raw Food) or prey-model raw diet. Although I was interested in feeding Zara a diet of whole foods when we first got her, I didn't feel up to the task at the time. But after a year of digestive problems, recurrent yeast infections, and trouble keeping weight on her, I was ready to try it.

I thought that preparing the raw diet myself was the only option, but after visiting a locally owned Raleigh pet store, I discovered that there were multiple commercially prepared raw products on the market. I bought several bags of frozen raw patties and decided to switch Zara right away. It was pricey, but her health was important.

I saw almost instant results. Zara's stools became firmer and smaller, and she started pooping only twice a day instead of four or five times. She gained weight and maintained it. After a few weeks, she shed a lot of hair, and then her coat was softer and shinier. She stopped getting yeast infections in her ears, and her feet lost the "Frito feet" smell that many owners experience.

I was thrilled. Since the premade raw was so expensive, after a few months, I decided to try the DIY version. This cut my costs in half. I soon discovered that prepping her food myself wasn't that much extra work. I shopped at a nearby Asian grocery store and a local meat market to find the "off cuts" that were required, such as liver, kidney, feet, tongue, hearts, and lung. After being on the premade raw for four months, Zara transitioned to DIY raw seamlessly. The integration of raw, edible bones eventually cleaned the plaque off her teeth that had built up since she was a puppy.

That summer, in between my obsessive internet searches and learning how to prepare her food, I started training Zara to be a therapy dog. I had learned about therapy dogs when Zara was about a year old, and I thought that it would be a perfect job for her. She loved people and loved attention. I decided that it was time for her to finally earn the elusive Canine Good Citizen title and find out how to get certified as a therapy dog team. We found a dog trainer that offered a CGC class, which was a prerequisite to taking their Pet Therapy class, and signed up. It would be held outside at different parks throughout Raleigh. *We've got this*, I thought smugly. Zara was two-and-a-half and already an obedient dog. I figured we'd breeze through the CGC lessons. The training company had given me special permission to enter Zara into this Public Manners class. They typically required a class called Home Manners first, but given that Zara had taken several obedience classes already, they made an exception.

The first class was held on a Saturday in July. Chris and I went to the park and stood around in a circle with several other owners and their dogs. We practiced walking our dogs around in a circle with the others. Loose-leash walking was still not Zara's strong suit, and she was pulling on the leash, despite wearing a front-clip harness that was supposed to cut down on pulling. Then the trainer asked us to put our dogs in a sit, without using any treats. *Hmm*, I thought. Zara didn't like to do things like that without treats. Zara would not sit or lay down, or if she would, it was only for a second and then she'd pop right back up. Apparently, we had taught sit and down incorrectly. The trainer wanted the dogs to sit or lay down until you gave them a release word (like "free"). We had done a little bit of that when she was a puppy, but not much. We usually just had her sit and then gave her a reward almost immediately. Also, I typically didn't have Zara sit or down much in public. She would sit or down in the house without treats, but outside was a different story. She was distracted during that first class—looking at squirrels, chasing shadows, sniffing who knows what. Meanwhile, all the other dogs were calmly sitting or laying down (on concrete!) looking like angels. To make matters worse, many of them were puppies, whereas we were the ones with the supposedly well-trained two-and-a-half-year-old adult! I felt like we had failed the class already.

Over the next several weeks, we worked on Zara's leash-walking skills and having her sit until I gave a release command. I wasn't really worried about some of the other aspects of the test, like walking by other dogs or being greeted by a stranger. At the beginning of August, it was finally time to take the CGC test. It was held outside, at another park in Raleigh. This annoyed me, because a lot of CGC tests are held inside. While I recognize that a well-behaved dog should be fine inside or outside, it didn't seem fair that some dogs were judged indoors, which is much less distracting than an outside environment with squirrels running around and bugs flying by. Thankfully, Zara passed easily and finally earned her CGC title.

Next up was the Pet Therapy class. Taking a class is not required to become a therapy dog, but I figured it would be helpful. We worked on a lot of things that we covered in the Public Manners class—loose-leash walking, sit, down, stay, and behaving around other dogs. Zara and I continued to work on the loose-leash walking, and she was starting to show some improvement.

The instructors also had us practice "rough petting" of the dogs, and hugs, since patients or kids that you're visiting may not always pet the dog in a gentle way, or they may be somewhat uncoordinated or have jerky movements. Thankfully, Zara did not mind hugs like some dogs do. She sometimes hugged us!

We also spent a lot of time getting the dogs accustomed to crutches, a walker, and a wheelchair. Zara didn't mind the walker or the wheelchair too much, but she was really freaked out by the crutches at first. I don't think that she'd seen crutches before, and she didn't like the noise they made on the floor. But after laying them down flat on the ground, letting her sniff them, and praising her, she was less afraid.

The instructors talked a lot about how to interact with the patients, how to be respectful, and how to answer certain questions. I think it's easy to focus a lot of energy on training your dog, but as the handler, you are doing a lot of interacting with the patient as well.

I thought Zara did really well in the class. She was somewhat antsy at first, but I think that was because I didn't feed her dinner beforehand. Before the following classes, I made sure to feed her ahead of time, and she lay down on the towel I had brought and chilled out when we weren't doing active things.

Zara and I were certified as a therapy dog team in November of 2016. There are many different organizations that certify dogs to become therapy dogs, depending on where you live. I chose the Alliance of Therapy Dogs (ATD). We began doing visits at a local nursing home once a week.

Since moving to Raleigh, we had been spending a lot of time at the local dog park. Millbrook Dog Park was a three-acre fenced space with small baby pools, trees, open areas, and lots of tennis balls. When I visited with Zara in the mornings, there were only a few people and dogs. I enjoyed chatting with the other owners while Zara chased balls. In the afternoons, it was much more crowded, and Zara and I tried to seclude ourselves in a far corner away from the ruckus.

One day, I met a guy who had a young Brittany. We connected over our bird dogs and talked about how much energy they had. He told me that he was part of a group called NAVHDA, which helps people train their bird dogs. He also told me that he was trying to train his dog himself, and he had bought videos from a well-known kennel. In all of my research, I had heard of the training kennel, but I did not know anything about NAVHDA. He offered to let me borrow the videos.

I watched the videos over a period of several days, and took extensive notes. They explained how to properly introduce a puppy to birds, how to train "heel" and "come," and how to train your dog to be steady. I learned a lot watching the videos and I felt grateful that this opportunity had fallen into my lap. Maybe this was a sign that I could train Zara myself!

I also looked up NAVHDA. It is an acronym for the North American Versatile Hunting Dog Association and there were two chapters in North Carolina—both not too far away from where I lived in Raleigh. However, after seeing that NAVHDA's tests focused on water work and ducks, I concluded that it was not right for me. All I wanted was for Zara to be steady in the field. I didn't need to be doing all those other complicated tests.

I started following the method of teaching "whoa" that was described in the videos. This command is used in bird dog training to remind the dog to stay still when it finds a bird. "Whoa" means stand still and don't move until the handler releases you. When a pointing dog smells a game bird, such as a quail, their natural instinct is to freeze into an intense pointing stance. However, most dogs are not naturally "steady." Eventually, most dogs without any prior training will break their point and try to catch the bird, which will likely cause it to fly. Their other natural instinct is to chase the bird once it's in flight.

For advanced bird dog competitions, the dog must be trained to stay still until the handler releases it. As the dog is pointing, the handler will walk up and flush the bird, expecting the dog to remain in its original position as the bird takes off, regardless of whether it is shot or not. If the dog tries to creep forward or break their stance at any point, the handler can say "whoa," which, if trained properly, should stop the dog from any further movement. Training a dog to be steady like this usually takes a while, because the dog has a strong desire to move and/or chase.

However, I misunderstood how whoa should be used. I thought

that the handler would give a strong "whoa" as soon as the dog went on point and that command alone held enough power to keep the dog from moving. It wasn't until several years later when I found out that ideally you don't even need to say "whoa" if the dog is trained properly. It's more of a backup to reinforce what the dog already knows. At the time, this steadiness training seemed straightforward to me. I had no idea it would take years until Zara was reliably steady. I thought I'd have her ready to compete in a few months. Oh, how naïve I was!

The videos explained that you wanted to teach the command without any birds to begin with. Once the dog had a solid understanding of "whoa," it could be applied to situations with birds.

I started by putting Zara on a long leash, telling her "whoa" and trying to get her to stay in the same place. Although this method used an electronic collar to enforce whoa, I opted not to use one since I had scared Zara with it. I figured I didn't need it. I increased the difficulty by taking steps away from her, and gradually throwing objects around after I had given the command. I took her to various public parks around Raleigh to practice this. I had some success, but I was making it harder on myself by not using the e-collar. Also, I don't think I realized what a powerful stimulus birds are to a hunting dog and how being steady in parks was vastly different to being steady on a bird.

Chapter 9

The Search Continues

In January 2017, nine months after we had moved to Raleigh, I was still searching for a place to train Zara. I reached out to the contact person for the Sandhills Pointing Breeds Club (SPBC), which is an organization of bird dog owners that has a 100-acre property 90 minutes south of Raleigh. I had seen SPBC pop up in my internet searches before, but the long drive had turned me off. Without any viable closer options, I decided to check it out.

I met Richard "Ozzie" Osborne at SPBC on a cold day in late January. He showed me the grounds and told me about the club. The property was beautiful. It was much larger than the hunt club where I had gone with Kim. There were multiple fields, a pigeon coop, a quail coop, and a clubhouse. While we were there, Zara ran around the fields and pointed some quail that had been left over from an earlier training session.

Ozzie told me that in addition to being a club member, he also trained pointing dogs and would be happy to give Zara and me lessons. However, he trained dogs for hunting tests, not field trials. He preferred hunting tests since they are based on a standard and, every dog can pass if they do well. He explained that field trials are competitive events and don't simulate real hunting scenarios. He specifically trained dogs for AKC Master Hunter Tests, which are the highest level. He said that people usually had to pick one or the other—a dog that would hunt close to its owner for a hunting test would likely not do well in a field trial, where the judges were looking for them to run really far ahead of the handlers.

Since Master Hunting Tests involve retrieving, Ozzie said that all dogs needed to be "force fetched" to make them reliable retrievers. I had a vague idea of what force fetch was—again, I had done some internet research—and it typically involved pinching a dog's ear or pulling on one of their toes to get them to put an object in their mouth. Lots of repetitions eventually made a dog retrieve on command. As someone who had exclusively used positive reinforcement to train Zara and had scared her with the e-collar, the idea of force fetch made me cringe.

I left SPBC that day feeling confused. I loved the property and facilities offered to members; for $75 a year, it was a bargain. But I wasn't sure I could justify a three-hour round trip drive on a regular basis. Although I was working for myself and had a flexible schedule, it just seemed like too much.

As for everything Ozzie had said, I felt torn. For several months, I had been certain that AKC Walking Field Trials were what I wanted to do with Zara—they didn't involve retrieving, so it seemed like the easier route. But now I wasn't sure. If I wanted to train with him, I would have to commit to hunting tests.

I reached out to Laura Miller, the owner of Zara's sire, Bull. She mostly ran Bull in field trials, but I knew she had also done a few Master Hunting Tests with him. I wanted to see what she thought of this divide and whether I needed to choose.

Laura responded to my email, and we later talked on the phone. She confirmed that, yes, sometimes dogs were suited more toward one or the other. However, she said that plenty of field trial dogs pass hunting tests and some hunting test dogs do well in walking trials. She felt that hunting tests are more obedience-based, and a dog can be trained to do it, whereas field trials require a natural ability and show the instincts and intelligence of a bird dog.

She reminded me that Zara's hunting test judge from her first Junior Hunting Test called her after he judged Zara. He was ecstatic about her natural ability—that she searched objectives like a field trial dog and had the intelligence to do it herself. Objectives are places where birds are likely to be found. She also told me that Bull was a natural retriever, and she didn't have to do a lot of work to persuade him to retrieve birds. That was encouraging to hear, but I wasn't sure that Zara would be the same.

Laura suggested going to both field trials and hunting tests to spectate and learn more about them. I did go to the Conestoga Vizsla Club's Spring Field Trial in March 2017. It was a horseback trial, where handlers and judges ride on horses and the dogs run ahead. It was amazing how quickly and far they ran, but I couldn't see too much because I didn't want to ride a horse. After attending that event and talking to Laura, I emailed Ozzie and told him that I wanted to focus on training Zara for field trials. If Laura thought Zara had potential as a field trial dog, then I would continue on my course. I still didn't have a good plan, but I decided that SPBC was too far away, and I would keep looking for other options.

Chapter 10

A New Puppy

Since Zara was about a year old, Chris and I had talked about the possibility of getting another dog. We had dog-sat for other people's dogs multiple times by then and enjoyed how two dogs would tire each other out. Owning an energetic Vizsla was a lot of work. We thought that adding a second dog would help with this daily task.

I loved Zara and thought we should get another Vizsla. However, Chris was not on the same page. Even though he had originally wanted a Vizsla, after living with one, he did not want a second dog with the same amount of energy. This argument didn't make sense to me. We were already exercising Zara at a high level. Adding another Vizsla wouldn't change that. In fact, another Vizsla would fit right in!

Zara's breeder had another litter of puppies in August 2016. I tried to convince Chris to get another puppy from her, but he wasn't having it. So we started researching other breeds. We both liked the short hair of the Vizsla, but he wanted an even bigger dog and certainly one with less energy. That left relatively few options. We knew we had to get a dog that could at least keep up with Zara. Getting something like a lazy Bulldog or Pug would be a disaster. I could just imagine her barking at it incessantly, trying to get it to play with her.

Eventually, much like the way he had latched onto the Vizsla breed in 2012, Chris decided that a Rhodesian Ridgeback was the next dog for us. We had seen Ridgebacks at the dog park but didn't have much experience with them otherwise. Again, I was hesitant. Ridgebacks were bred from a variety of breeds in Zimbabwe in the late 1800s, including the Great Dane, Boerboel, and Greyhound, among others. They were bred to hunt large game, such as lions, and to be guard dogs and protectors of their families and property. When tracking large game, Ridgebacks hunted in packs and were expected to go out in front of the hunter, find a large animal, and keep the animal "at bay" until the hunter arrived to kill it. Because of this, Ridgebacks are much more independent-minded than Vizslas, which translates into "stubborn," less "eager to please," and potentially "harder to train."

That was my main concern. I was also not enthusiastic about the size. We knew we wanted a male dog, and male Ridgebacks are typically 80 to 90 pounds, or, potentially, even more. Zara was a very reasonable 46 pounds. I'm not a big person—I would only have 35 pounds on a large male Ridgeback. Zara had astounding strength when she felt like pulling. I could only imagine how strong a Ridgeback could be!

Despite all that, I was willing to consider a Ridgeback, so I began looking for breeders in the summer of 2016. Although I had stumbled onto a good breeder with Jane, I now knew the characteristics of a reputable breeder and was able to weed out the less desirable ones. I contacted a few in North Carolina and even spoke to one on the phone. Some had wait lists nearly two years long, and we learned from another source that one of the breeders I'd reached out to had had issues with hypothyroidism in her lines. No thanks. Since we had only recently moved to Raleigh, we still felt very connected to the DC area, and Chris was regularly traveling back there for work. I expanded my search to Northern Virginia and located Carrie Ellingson of Adriatic Ridgebacks. She was planning a litter in the spring of 2017. She was involved in conformation shows and was also a raw feeder! It was a good match, and we got on her list.

We already had the Ridgeback's name picked out: Colombo. Although it was a bit long, I knew that we'd shorten it and come up with multiple nicknames. Colombo's litter was born on April 13, 2017, and he came home with us at the end of June. At 10 weeks, he was already more than 20 pounds with massive paws. I knew he was going to be a big boy.

Colombo loved Zara instantly and was obsessed with following her around, playing with her, and tormenting her. Zara, on the other hand, was not pleased. She was already three-and-half and did not like over-enthusiastic puppies. She made it known from day one that she was the queen, and he needed to learn his place. Colombo didn't seem to mind, though. She'd tell him off with a snap or bared teeth, but he'd just come back for more. Zara bore most of the brunt of the puppy teeth and shark attacks when Colombo was young.

After a few weeks, Zara began to allow him to play with her more, although it was always on her terms. Sometimes she would look at me, and it seemed like she was saying, "Why did you get this baby shark to torment me?" By that point, Zara was very well-behaved and such a sweet dog. Having a three-year-old dog was fairly easy. I worried that adding this new puppy would upset the equilibrium.

But gradually Colombo grew on Zara, and she began to accept him. I noticed that she really started to love him when he was about 10 months, and finally getting out of the annoying puppy stage. They'd engage in elaborate licking rituals, and she seemed to fully enjoy playing with him. But as Colombo got older, Zara remained the top dog, even though he soon doubled her in weight.

The differences between a Ridgeback and a Vizsla became apparent already when Colombo was young. He was much slower-moving and contemplative than Zara was as a puppy. Zara had been nonstop. Almost every photo I have of her as a baby is blurry. If I asked him to do something, he'd sit and think about it for a minute before complying. He loved to sunbathe on the deck and watch Zara zoom around the half-acre yard of the house Chris and I had bought in Raleigh that spring. He also grew very quickly, and, by four months or so, was nearly Zara's size.

Despite the distraction of a new puppy, I had not forgotten about trying to train Zara for hunting. By the summer of 2017, I was getting frustrated and was not sure how feasible it was going to be for me to train Zara myself. I was still trying to work on "whoa," but without access to birds, how would I ever get her ready to compete?

I recalled my conversations with the guy at the dog park the previous summer and remembered that there were two NAVHDA chapters in North Carolina. *Maybe I should give them a shot*, I thought. My searches for other breed clubs and bird dog training clubs was turning up nothing. I looked on NAVHDA's website and saw that the Tarheel Chapter was having a training day the first weekend of August. I sent the guy I'd met at the dog park a Facebook message to find out more about his NAVHDA experience. He assured me that the Tarheel Chapter was a group of friendly people and encouraged me to go check it out. I also messaged the chapter on their Facebook page and told them that I planned to attend.

On Saturday, August 5th, I drove the hour and fifteen minutes from my house to Lillington, North Carolina, a small town south of Raleigh. Zara was in the back seat wearing her blaze orange collar. Blaze orange is the color worn by hunters to be visible while hunting. At least she would fit in. I, on the other hand, had on running shorts, a race shirt I'd gotten from a triathlon, and bright pink knee-high Hunter rain boots, which I figured made the most sense, since I didn't know what the grounds would be like.

Driving onto the property, I passed a beautiful lake and fields. I reached the end of the driveway and parked next to the other cars, but I immediately felt nervous and out-of-place. Almost everyone had some form of pickup truck. There were small pickup trucks, ones with double wheels in the back, and ones with covered beds. Most of them had one or more fancy crates tied down in the back with dogs inside. One guy's truck had a truck cap covering the bed, with dog crates and stuff inside, a roof rack that held a kayak, a small trailer attached to the back with an ATV on it, and a hitch haul attached to the front with a bird box strapped on it. Meanwhile, I was driving my tiny Honda Fit hatchback with my dog sitting in the back seat, unrestrained. *Wow, where am I?* I thought, feeling intimidated.

After I got Zara out of the car and walked her around a little bit, one of the women called everyone to form a circle. About 20 people had showed up, a good mix of men and women. Everyone gathered around, and the woman, who introduced herself as the chapter secretary, welcomed us and explained that since there were a lot of new people, we were going to go around the circle and introduce ourselves, our dog, and what our goals were. People started introducing themselves, talking about NA and UT tests, and it seemed like everyone had a "Draht," whatever kind of dog that was. When it was my turn, I explained that I was new to NAVHDA but had run Zara in AKC Junior Hunting Tests. I said that I wanted to get her steady in the field to run field trials.

After the introductions, we broke up into groups. The people who had younger dogs went off together, and the people who were training for an event called the Invitational went somewhere else. That left me with the "UT" people. Some of them went into the field. I hung around the pond, watching a guy named Andrew shoot a bumper launcher into the water. I'd never seen a bumper launcher before. It was a soft canvas bumper toy attached to a metal piece that you pulled back to release it. The bumper flew out a long distance into the pond, and a blank gunshot was fired.

Andrew's dog, which he told me was a Deutsch Drahthaar, sat patiently on the bank as he shot the bumper into the water. After it landed with a small splash, he gave her a release command, and she bounded into the water. She swam directly to the bumper, picked it up, and swam back to him. When she reached the bank, she slowly walked toward him, sat squarely next to him, and presented the bumper. After he took it from her, she shook on command. *Wow*, I thought. *Zara would never do that!* Even though she liked to retrieve toys, she definitely did not bring them to hand.

Andrew gave Zara a chance to retrieve the bumper. She swam out and picked it up, but dropped it as soon as she got to the shore, getting distracted by the little fish swimming around. "She doesn't retrieve to hand," I said apologetically, picking up the bumper myself. Andrew didn't seemed fazed.

Later that morning, I had the chance to take her into the field to hunt some quail. I don't remember the details of the experience, but I know I went into the field with only one other guy, telling him that Zara didn't need anyone to shoot birds for her, because she was not going to retrieve them. He seemed a bit confused by this, but obliged. I asked him to shoot my blank pistol when the birds flew instead. I'm sure she pointed well, and then tried to chase the birds, without showing much indication of steadiness. We had a long way to go, although I didn't realize it then.

Years later, it occurred to me that most people in my position would have cut their losses and gotten a new puppy to learn with. I saw this when new people would show up to our NAVHDA training days, a three- or four-year-old dog in tow. When asked about their dog's abilities, they would shrug dismissively and say, "Oh, she's not steady. But I'm getting a new puppy in a few months."

Getting a new puppy in order to start with a clean slate never even crossed my mind. I already had a talented dog, why did I need another one? The whole reason I wanted to get involved in bird dog training was to learn *with Zara*. I had no interest if she was not involved. The fact that she was approaching four years old did not deter me at all. In retrospect, it was probably for the best that our second dog was a Rhodesian Ridgeback. If we had gotten another Vizsla in 2017 instead, I would have been just like those other people. It would have been easy to cast Zara aside and focus on training the new puppy from the beginning.

By the time I left that day, I was impressed with what I'd seen. Joining NAVHDA would give me a chance to train with live birds every month, and all of the chapter members I had met were welcoming and friendly, even to someone who clearly looked like an outsider. But I wasn't going to involve myself in all of the water work and whatever else was required for the UT Test, I decided. I would use NAVHDA to get Zara steady in the field so I could run her in AKC Field Trials.

Chapter 11

Giving NAVHDA a Try

That fall, I joined the Tarheel Chapter and attended their training days at the beginning of September and October. I liked that everyone was approachable and willing to share their knowledge with me. At one of the first training days, I met Steve Greger, who is a Senior Judge for NAVHDA. I told him we were working on steadiness, and he recommended teaching Zara "whoa" on a table or raised platform. "Tell her whoa," he said. "If she moves, just pick her up and put her back where she was." This technique seemed easy enough and gave me a way to correct her without using the e-collar. So over the next several months, I started teaching Zara whoa by putting her on top of the covered hot tub in our backyard. We did this most mornings. As soon as she moved, I'd pick her up and set her back in place. I added distractions like walking away, throwing objects, and increased the duration that she had to stay. Taking Steve's suggestion, I eventually bought a toy called a "Tim bird," which is a plastic bird toy that you wind up and it flies off, similar to a real bird. Since we were living in a suburban neighborhood, I was enthusiastic about these sort of unconventional workarounds. I eventually moved to her being on the ground and then expanded to locations outside of my backyard.

I was consistent in my training, and this time I saw better results than when I had tried the previous year. Zara didn't like to be picked up, so that correction seemed to be enough to get the point across about what she was supposed to do. She was a pretty obedient dog and was willing to work with me. She wasn't trying to disobey me on purpose. But learning takes time, and teaching her "whoa" was not a quick process. I didn't use anything stronger, such as the e-collar. At that point, I was still only using the e-collar for recall and solely used the tone function.

As I started attending NAVHDA training days, I began to learn more about NAVHDA's testing system. There are three main levels of tests. The Natural Ability (NA) test is designed for puppies up to 16 months of age. They are evaluated on three activities: field work, swimming, and a pheasant track. In the field portion, the dogs have to show the ability to search, find birds, and point. They don't have to demonstrate any steadiness, and the birds are not shot. While they are running ahead hunting, two shots are fired to make sure they aren't gun shy. The field work in the NA test is similar to the Junior Hunter level of AKC Hunting Tests, although the dogs are run alone, without a bracemate.

The water portion consists of the handler throwing bumpers into a pond twice to see the dog swim. This shows they have the desire to go into the water away from the handler. Bumpers are typically plastic cylindrical training toys with a thin rope on the end. The rope makes them easy to throw a long distance. Finally, the puppies are evaluated on their ability to follow the scent track of a live pheasant that has been released in a field and run into cover.

NAVHDA's finished gun dog test is called the Utility Test (UT). This consists of four parts. In the field, the dog hunts for 30 minutes and is expected to find birds, point, and remain steady through the shot and fall of the bird. All of the birds are shot if it is safe to do so. The dog must retrieve to the handler's hand without dropping the bird.

The second land portion is a duck drag. A judge places a few duck feathers on the ground, and then drags a dead duck about 100–150 yards across a field. After dropping off the duck, he or she hides to observe what the dog will do when it encounters the duck. The handler brings the dog up to the feather pile, gives one command, and the dog is expected to follow the track and bring the duck back to the handler. This section demonstrates the dog's obedience and willingness to execute a command when it is out of sight of the handler.

The next part is the heeling/remaining by the blind/steady by the blind/retrieve of dead duck sequence. The handler and dog must heel together for approximately 50 yards. Heeling means that the dog should be walking right next to the handler, not in front of or behind them. The dog cannot be pulling on the leash. After that, the handler positions the dog inside a folded blind or screen at the edge of a pond and gives them a whoa or stay command. The handler then goes out of sight of the dog and fires two blank shots. The handler returns to the dog, and repositions them outside of the blind and facing the pond. The handler and a helper fire a series of distraction shots. Lastly, a dead duck is launched from the shoreline, and the dog is sent to retrieve it from the middle of the pond. The duck must be brought back to hand.

The last part of the Utility Test is the duck search. According to the NAVHDA *Aims, Programs, Test Rules* booklet, during the test, "with dog and handler both out of sight, a healthy pen-raised mallard...is rendered flightless...One of the Judges will toss the duck out well into or past the cover at the edge of the water...the handler and dog are called up and the dog is placed in position off-lead...The handler will fire one blank shot over the water and send the dog...The capable dog will systematically search likely cover and...will find and follow the scent path left as the duck moves through the aquatic cover and over stretches of open water. If the scent is lost, the dog should not mill around aimlessly at the spot, but should start a systematic search to relocate the scent. Each dog is allowed approximately 10 minutes to search out the duck...If the opportunity for a retrieve occurs, such as the duck being caught or shot, the retrieve must be successfully completed."[2]

Some of the more important aspects of a successful duck search are independence (the ability of the dog to go away and out of sight of the handler) and an expanding search. The dog shouldn't focus on a small area of the pond. Once an area is thoroughly checked, the dog should keep expanding their search to a wider/further area.

NAVHDA also has a simpler version of the Utility Test, called the Utility Preparatory Test (UPT) that has slightly less strict criteria. However, not as many people enter this level.

A dog can earn a Prize 1 (highest), Prize 2, or Prize 3 in NA, UPT, and UT if they pass. If they don't pass, they receive a score of "no prize." There are multiple criteria that are scored by the judges and there are minimum scores that have to be obtained in order to receive a certain prize. Each criteria is scored from 0 to 4. For example, a dog needs a 4 in

---

2   The full NAVHDA *Aims, Programs, Test Rules* booklet is available at
    https://www.navhda.org/aims-programs-test-rules/

Duck Search, Pointing, Use of Nose, and Desire to Work in order to earn a Prize 1 in the Utility Test. If a dog does earn a Prize 1, they qualify for the highest level of NAVHDA's tests: the Invitational.

The Invitational is held once a year and moves around the country. It is typically a four-day event. At the Invitational, there are four main portions: a one-hour field work session, where the dog is run with a bracemate, a 100-yard blind retrieve across water, a double-marked retrieve, consisting of two ducks being thrown into a large pond, an honor of another dog's water retrieve, and off-leash heeling. The Invitational is pass/fail, and a dog that passes earns the title of Versatile Champion (VC).

When I first joined NAVHDA, Zara was too old for the Natural Ability Test. So I spent most of my time with the other members who were training for Utility. It seemed really involved. In fact, the first time I went to one of the Tarheel Chapter's tests and witnessed it, I was surprised by how low the scores were for dogs that I thought had done a great job. Even though I was mainly interested in competing in field trials, during the training days, I would join in when people were practicing other parts of the test besides field work. One aspect that Zara and I tried early on was the heeling/remaining by the blind/steady by the blind sequence.

The heeling part of this exercise was a disaster. Zara was pulling hard on her leash every time I tried it, because she was so anxious to get to the water. She must have sensed that something exciting was about to happen. Although it was embarrassing to have her yanking me along while everyone else's dog walked calmly by their side, I couldn't blame her, because I'd never taught her to heel. We'd gotten to the point where she'd walk relatively calmly while wearing a front-clip harness. But she was a different animal wearing a regular collar. At the training days, none of the other dogs were wearing a harness, so I was embarrassed to have Zara sport one.

Surprisingly, the remaining by the blind part was relatively easy for her. By that point, she was four years old, and I had been drilling "stay" and later, "whoa," into her for a long time. She was able to stay while I went out of sight to fire the blank shots. I returned to her to complete the sequence. Instead of a duck, we used a duck-shaped training toy, called a dokken, to throw into the lake. She went into the water after the launched duck toy, although she would not bring it back to me. She dropped it at the shore line and started looking for fish.

The other thing Zara had a chance to do was the duck search. During one training day, we drove to a nearby swamp with several other people. One of the guys pulled the flight feathers from a live duck and released it into the swamp using a kayak. Then another handler brought his dog up to the bank of the swamp, fired a blank gunshot, and released his dog. The dog took off swimming in search of the duck. Eventually, the dog found the duck and brought it back to the handler. At the time, I didn't really understand the intricacies of the duck search. It seemed that if your dog had the desire and instinct to search for ducks, you were good to go.

The first time Zara tried a duck search, I was pleased with how she performed. As soon as I released her, she swam out into the pond and started searching around. By this point, she loved being in the water and was a strong swimmer, so that helped. Zara stayed in the swamp for about 10 minutes without coming back to me. At one point, she found the duck and started chasing it. The guys who were observing encouraged me to tell her to fetch it. "She's not going to pick it up," I said, knowing full well that she didn't retrieve birds. I shouted for her to fetch it anyway. She did not. She lost sight of the duck once it dove into the water, and I called her back to me soon after that.

That fall, I had gotten proof that Zara did not want to retrieve birds. While conducting one of my internet searches to find a place to train, I had come across the Tarheel Weimaraner Club. Weimaraners are a similar breed to Vizslas, although their fur is entirely gray instead of rust. The club was having a training day in September in preparation for a Weimaraner-specific "retrieving ratings" test that fall. Figuring it couldn't hurt to ask, I emailed the organizer and asked if Zara and I could attend this event, even though she was a Vizsla. The woman wrote me back and invited me to come out.

I went to their event in mid-September. It was held on a farm about 40 minutes from my house, and everyone else there had a Weimaraner. I certainly got some weird looks. Surprisingly, most of the other handlers were women. Most hunting events I'd attended had a majority of men. The club had a designated shooting area set up in a clearing in the woods. Each handler brought their dog up to the clearing and positioned the dog next to them. A less-experienced dog remained on a leash, while a fully trained, "finished" gun dog sat off-leash next to the handler. One person released a live pigeon, and it flew to the middle of the clearing, where another person shot it with a shotgun. The dog was expected to remain seated until the bird fell and the handler sent it to retrieve. I watched a couple of the advanced dogs do this sequence and, after being released, they promptly ran to the bird, picked it up, and returned to their handlers, sitting nicely next to them with the bird in their mouths. It looked easy enough.

When it was Zara's turn, she enthusiastically pulled me toward the retrieving area. I tried to get to her walk politely on the leash, but we were still years away from mastering heeling. It was a lost cause without her harness. I held her collar while the bird was being shot. I knew she was not steady yet. Once the bird fell, I released her, telling her to "get it!" She ran right toward the bird. *That's a good sign!* I thought. But instead of picking it up, she just stared at it, like she was pointing it. "Zara, get it!" I called. "Come on, get it!"

She continued to stare at the dead bird. I sighed, and walked over to where she was standing. "Get it, Zar!" She wagged her tail. I picked up the dead pigeon, and clipped the leash to her collar.

Afterwards, one of the women in the club encouraged me to shake the dead pigeon around in front of Zara to increase her excitement. I tried it, flapping the bird in front of her face and making high-pitched noises. "Get it, Zara! Get it get it get it!" I exclaimed. She looked excited and tentatively opened her mouth but was unwilling to grab it. I tried a few more times with similar results.

"It's okay," I said to the woman, shrugging my shoulders. "We'll have to work on it." At this point, I was not particularly concerned that she wouldn't retrieve. I had just joined NAVHDA, and I knew that most field trials didn't require retrieving.

Chapter 12

Retrieve Training

In January 2018, the NAVHDA training day fell on a bitterly cold Saturday. Everyone was bundled up in insulated camouflage attire, which I assumed they wore hunting in the winter. I had an old coat that I wore around the yard when I was out with the dogs, but I felt embarrassed to wear it because it was bulky and bright purple. I still felt like an outsider; I didn't need my apparel to confirm it. Wearing that coat to a training day would not bother me now, but at the time, I was trying to blend in, not stand out. Instead, I borrowed Chris' old ski jacket, which was orange, so at least the color fit. I paired it with a worn pair of jeans. I didn't have any clothing specifically for hunting.

That morning, Scott Caldwell, who is a dog trainer, breeder, and owner of Rusty Guns Kennel, which is where the Tarheel Chapter trains, gave a demonstration on the force fetch process. Several of us gathered around a low table he had set up underneath a tree. He explained how force fetch uses a "pressure on/pressure off" technique to compel the dog to put something in its mouth. When pressure is applied, the dog eventually learns to get the object in its mouth as quickly as possible to turn the pressure off. He used one of his German Shorthaired Pointers to demonstrate. She was sitting at one end of the table. He placed a bumper at the other end. He showed us how to firmly press a section of the dog's ear between our thumb and forefinger to apply pressure. Then he said "fetch." She quickly walked down the length of the table and picked up the bumper. Once it was in her mouth, Scott released his grip on her ear.

I watched this process quietly, taking it in. I was glad to see it explained in more detail than I had read online. The pressure on/pressure off concept made sense to me. I still didn't think it was something I wanted to do with Zara, but it was good to have the knowledge in my back pocket.

Around the same time, I was actively preparing to enter my first conformation show with Colombo. I had known next to nothing about showing dogs before we got him, but we had agreed to show him to his championship, and I wanted to learn how to handle him myself.

Conformation is a dog sport that judges purebred dogs on how closely they match the breed standard. The dogs run around a ring with their handlers, are examined by a judge, and if they win, can earn points toward a championship or grand championship. Only intact animals are eligible for conformation shows because the original purpose of the sport was to evaluate dogs for breeding. Spayed and neutered dogs are not eligible for AKC conformation events, although they can compete in other types of shows, such as those put on by the United Kennel Club (UKC).

Colombo was not a natural show dog. By the time we started handling classes when he was five months old, he did not like being touched by other people and was terrified of the instructors. He would barely let me stack him, which is the process of arranging a show dog's body into the proper position. Perhaps I should have done more with him when he was really young. We had socialized him thoroughly, I thought. We had done a puppy kindergarten class starting when he was 12 weeks old, introducing basic commands, clicker training, and some puppy playtime with other young dogs. I had made a point to take him to dog-friendly stores like Home Depot and Dick's Sporting Goods to have people pet him. That summer, we'd gone on a two-week road trip to Maine, and he'd experienced the beach, plenty of kids, friends' houses, a ride on an antique trolley car, hotels, camping, and city life. Maybe the reluctance to show was just his personality.

Regardless, I carried on, attending handling classes and trying to get him to enjoy it. By January, we were finally ready for his first conformation show. He was nine months old, weighed 70 pounds, and looked like a skinny teenage boy. Given that he would eventually top out at 95 pounds at three years old, it's no wonder he didn't win anything in the first year.

We traveled to Richmond, Virginia for the show and met up with Colombo's breeder and the owner of one of his sisters. The show was quick, over in less than an hour, and Colombo earned second place out of the two dogs in his class. But it went well: he wasn't nervous and did allow the judge to touch him without freaking out.

I had thought that I wouldn't like dog shows, because so many people I knew talked negatively about them. They complained about having to dress up and the politics of judges picking professional handlers over amateur owner handlers. But surprisingly, I discovered that I loved it.

I enjoyed dressing up, the atmosphere, the efficiency, being around other dog people, and having fun with my dog. It didn't matter to me that Colombo didn't win. I had learned a new sport, and I had fun practicing my new skills. Besides doing the Junior Hunting Tests with Zara, this was my first foray into dog sports, and I was beginning to discover how much I loved competing.

During the spring of 2018, I was still working on teaching Zara the "whoa" command. I did a few minutes of training each morning, and she seemed to be understanding what it meant. Zara was off the hot tub and on the ground. When I went to the NAVHDA training days, I would tell her "whoa" after she went on point. I would have someone loop a leash under her belly to reinforce the command. That way, if she tried to move, which she usually did, she'd be restrained by the leash. In retrospect, this wasn't the most efficient method to use, but I didn't know any other way to do it. I'm not sure why I didn't watch videos or read books about how to teach steadiness. I guess I thought I had already done that (like when I watched the videos I borrowed), and this method was good enough. It's also likely I had not spent enough time proofing "whoa" without birds before I tried to use it around birds.

Other than that, I wasn't doing much with her training. I was enjoying attending the NAVHDA events, but I hadn't committed to testing her in their system, and I still felt like somewhat of an outsider. Competing in field trials also seemed like a faraway goal.

In June, I was browsing on Instagram and found the profile of a young woman who owned a German Shorthaired Pointer (GSP), fed her dogs a raw diet, and was a member of NAVHDA. She also lived in the Raleigh area. Intrigued, I messaged her. I was still looking to connect with other like-minded dog owners in the area. The fact that she was also interested in doing hunting events with her dog was a bonus.

We messaged and agreed to meet up at a local hiking trail. Emily had two dogs: a one-year-old GSP named Blitz and a five-year-old rescue Pitbull named Pinky. She was a dog obedience trainer and worked for a company that specialized in off-leash and electronic collar training. Like me, she had gotten her GSP without the intention of hunting with her, but very quickly realized how interesting it was. At the suggestion of Blitz's breeder, she had joined the Carolinas NAVHDA Chapter, which was the other chapter in North Carolina, and was preparing to test Blitz at the Natural Ability level in the fall.

With our shared interests, we quickly became friends and met up regularly to hike with our dogs. I was excited to hang out with someone who was close in age to me and also shared my interest in NAVHDA and bird dogs.

That summer, I decided to try my hand at teaching Zara to retrieve. After being in NAVHDA for a year, I had begun to understand the importance of retrieving. I didn't know if it would work, but I figured I would give it a shot. She was four-and-a-half years old and had built up years of bad habits. When she was younger, we had always scolded her for picking up objects that didn't belong to her and had always commanded her to drop an object before we threw it. I now understood that we should have done the opposite: to always encourage her to hold objects and carry them until we took them from her. She also had never had a bird in her mouth.

I was hesitant to try the force fetch method that Scott had demonstrated. I wanted to do a more reward-based method if possible. I had been watching some YouTube videos by a Labrador Retriever owner who was training his dogs to fetch and hold bumpers without any physical pressure. He would gently open the dog's mouth and place the bumper inside, telling the dog to "hold." This seemed more up my alley. At that point, Zara had been completely trained using treats and praise.

The guy on YouTube had a table in his basement where he would place his dogs during their retrieving sessions. Many trainers use a table in the beginning, because the dog has a defined place where they cannot escape, and it's easier to access them because they're at eye level. Since I didn't have a suitable table, I just had Zara sit on the couch.

I held a bumper in one hand and opened her mouth with the other. I placed the bumper inside. I stroked her chin, telling her "Hold... hold." She did not look thrilled but was clearly not in any pain. After a few seconds of that, I clicked the clicker and said, "Give." She instantly dropped the bumper in my hand and looked for her treat. We did this for about five minutes, then stopped. I knew training sessions like this should be short and sweet.

I repeated this off and on for a few weeks. I incorporated the fetch command at the beginning of the sequence. I would say, "Fetch!" and offer Zara the bumper. However, she never wanted to take it in her mouth. I would still have to open her mouth and place it inside. After several sessions, it did seem like she was understanding what "hold" meant. I increased the duration that she had to hold it.

Watching YouTube videos was clearly not going to be enough to get me through this process. Even though my natural tendency was to do things on my own, I knew I needed help. I decided to reach out to Emily since I knew she had taught her GSP how to retrieve without using the traditional force fetch method. I told Emily that I was attempting to teach Zara how to fetch using positive reinforcement, but she didn't want to grab the bumper. She suggested that I wave the bumper around and use the excitement in my voice to get her amped and then want to put it in her mouth. She said to click as soon as she grabbed it, to clearly indicate that the word "fetch" meant grab the object.

I tried this, and it worked better. "Ready, Zara?" I'd say. "Ready, ready, ready?!" I'd tease her with the bumper and shake it. This must have activated something inside her, because her pupils dilated and she made a hesitant grab at it. "Yes!" I cried, and clicked as soon as the bumper was halfway in her jaws. The treat followed.

I did more sessions like that inside my house. I wasn't in a hurry, so I did them when I could. After Zara became a little more excited about taking the bumper from me, I would make her hold it for a few seconds until I clicked and gave her a treat. The "fetch" command was immediately followed by "hold." Next, after she had the bumper in her mouth, I tried to get her to walk next to me while holding it. She dropped it as soon as she started moving the first few times. But I would put it back in her mouth and encourage her to keep moving. The only correction she would receive for not taking the bumper or dropping it was a verbal "no," and then I'd try again.

By this point, it was October. I moved our training sessions outside, and I tried to do them consistently each weekday morning in my yard. Next, I threw the bumper a short distance and told her, "Fetch!" The motion of throwing usually made her want to get it. She had always enjoyed chasing after toys we threw. A lot of times she would drop the bumper on the way back, though, and I had to pick it up and put it back in her mouth. I eventually got her to hold it by immediately starting to walk around as soon as she got back to me. She was distracted enough by the sudden movement that she held onto it and followed me around. I was thrilled and had Chris film her doing this. A lot of times I filmed our training sessions, mainly so I could go back and see what I needed to improve. Since Chris was rarely outside with me during this time, I usually set up my phone in selfie mode on the ground. They were not high-quality videos, but they worked.

I started using other objects as well. I had the duck dokken and a thin piece of PVC pipe. The dokken was important to use, because in NAVHDA's Utility Test, three of the four sections involve retrieving a duck. A duck is much larger than a quail or chukar, so I knew I had to get her comfortable retrieving a larger object. In the beginning, I could tell that getting the dokken was not her favorite thing. I still wasn't sure I would enter Zara in the Utility Test, but the idea was growing on me.

Throughout the fall, I continued the process. I would sometimes send my videos to Emily to get suggestions on how to improve. After throwing the object, she advised placing it between Zara and me and asking her to fetch, in hopes that she might be more inclined to bring it right to me. I found that backing up as she was coming towards me helped with that. At this stage, I was not particular about how she held onto the bumper or dokken or her placement next to me when she delivered it. Holding onto one end was fine, as long as she didn't drop it. Typically, people want their retrievers to hold an object (and eventually, a dead bird) right in the middle with a balanced grip. This helps them to keep from dropping it and also makes it easier to carry across land or water. I figured I would clean that up later.

At the beginning of 2019, I had made a lot of progress with Zara. She now understood what fetch and hold meant and would generally pick up a select set of objects when asked, as long as I rewarded her with a treat afterwards. It had been about six months since I had first introduced the hold command, and we had taken things slowly. By then, I knew that I would have to find a way to enforce fetch. There were times during our training sessions when she'd get distracted and not want to fetch. I couldn't have that in a test. The whole point of teaching her to fetch was to get her reliable as close to 100% of the time as possible.

I knew that I didn't want to use the ear pinch unless I had to, but I was open to experimenting with the electronic collar. I talked to Emily about this, and she had done something similar with her young GSP. Since I had never used more than the tone function with Zara, I knew I would have to condition her to what the stimulation meant before applying it to the fetch command. Emily explained that I needed to use it on commands that Zara already knew, such as sit and come. The technique is to give a command, apply pressure (e-collar stimulation), and, as soon as the dog completes the command, the pressure comes off. They eventually learn to turn the pressure off by quickly completing the command.

This time, I used the lowest level with Zara (1 out of 18), since I knew she would feel the continuous stimulation even at this level. I fastened the e-collar around her neck and got the controller. We went outside and I asked her to sit. I pressed the continuous stimulation button and applied the pressure. She looked terrified and wasn't sure what to do. It was as if the stimulation had paralyzed her. "Zara, sit," I said again. I continued to hold down the continuous stimulation button. She tentatively sat. As soon as her butt hit the ground, I released the button on the e-collar remote. "Good girl!" I cried, offering her a treat. She took it, but did not look happy.

I decided we would do three reps during this training session. I knew it was better to keep it short, especially since Zara did not seem enthusiastic. I asked her to sit again, and pressed the stimulation button. Again, she hesitated, looking scared. I didn't understand why she wouldn't just sit down. I continued to encourage her to sit, and, eventually she did. As soon as she sat, I stopped the pressure. The third repetition went similarly. Afterwards, I praised and petted her and then exclaimed, "Where's your ball? Let's go get your ball!"

Once Zara realized that the training session was over, she perked up and ran across the yard, looking for her ball. I felt relieved that she was able to recover quickly. Introducing the e-collar turned out to be the hardest part of the training for me, because I didn't like the idea that I might be hurting her. I continued the process over the next several weeks, using the e-collar with sit and come. I also introduced the "place" command, which I had never taught her before. Place is used to get a dog to go onto a raised platform or bed and stay there until released. It's a very handy command and can be used inside the house as well as outside.

After a while, I felt that Zara gained more of an understanding of the pressure on/pressure off concept, but she never got to the point where I would say she understood it completely. It was probably my fault. Maybe I wasn't clear in my delivery when I was giving her commands, or maybe she had trouble understanding the concept because she was five years old. Typically, people e-collar condition their dogs when they're a lot younger, perhaps between six and 18 months.

At the same time I was teaching Zara what the e-collar pressure meant on commands she already knew, I started introducing dead birds during our fetch training sessions. From previous NAVHDA training days, I had a stash of frozen quail, chukar, and ducks in my garage freezer. A few days before the February NAVHDA training day, I defrosted a quail overnight. The next morning, I brought it outside, along with my clicker and bag of treats. I grabbed my camera too, so I could get a few photos if she was willing to retrieve it. I had to maintain her Instagram account, after all. "Ready, Zara?" I said. She jumped up to sniff the quail in my hand. "Ooh, you want this?" I asked with excitement in my voice. Her ears perked up. I sat my camera on the ground in our backyard where we did most of our training. "Ready? Fetch!" I threw the quail about 20 feet away from me.

Zara bounded after the quail and sniffed it when she got to it. "Good girl!" I encouraged. "Fetch!" She carefully picked it up and came back to me. "Good girl!" I exclaimed. I motioned to my right side. "With me. Hold." She sat next to me, still holding the quail. "Good girl." I reached down to take the quail from her. I clicked the clicker and said, "Give." She released the quail.

"What a good girl!" I cried and quickly rewarded her with some treats. I tossed the quail a few more times, and she picked it up. I was even able to get a photo of her holding it. We did a few more sessions with dead quail that week. I was hoping that maybe this would translate into her picking up a freshly shot bird during the training day.

That Saturday, we headed south to Lillington. It was a beautiful sunny day, with temperatures in the 30s in the morning, eventually peaking to the low 60s by afternoon. This was not unusual for winter in North Carolina. When it was time for Zara to go into the field, several other NAVHDA members came along—two gunners, a woman who was going to help me restrain Zara when I flushed the bird, and a few others who wanted to watch. I asked one of them to take a video for me. There were four quail planted in the field.

Unfortunately, there was only one opportunity for a retrieve. The first two quail that Zara found flew into the woods, and the gunners were unable to shoot them. The third bird seemed to have gotten up and moved, since we couldn't find it. On the last quail, Zara pointed, and my helper looped a leash under her belly to hold her back in case she decided to break. I moved in front of her to flush the bird. The gunners were ready. The quail started running, so I chased after it and managed to kick it into the air. The gunners fired their shotguns, but they weren't entirely sure that they'd hit it. Since Zara had stayed relatively steady throughout the whole sequence, they suggested I send her to retrieve to see if she could find it.

I walked back to Zara and said, "Fetch!" She bounded off to the edge of the woods. Everything had happened so quickly, and I had not been watching where the bird landed. All of sudden, I saw Zara emerge from the woods with the quail in her mouth! I was so surprised that you can hear the octave change in my voice in the video. "Good girl!" I cried. "Good girl!" I couldn't believe it. My hard work was paying off!

Zara headed towards me and then set the quail down about halfway. I walked over to her, picked up the quail and encouraged her to hold it in her mouth again. She took it, and then I gave her the release command. "This is the first time she's ever picked up a shot bird!" I told the other

NAVHDA members. Many of them had watched Zara in the field before and knew that she wouldn't retrieve. Instead, she would run to the dead bird and stare at it.

"Well, that's a case of beer!" Steve Greger said. He was serving as one of the gunners. "Firsts like that deserve buying a case of beer." I laughed. I would not buy a case of beer, but the joy I felt watching Zara retrieve her first shot bird was enough.

Chapter 13

Working Hard

At the beginning of April 2019, the Tarheel Chapter began taking entries for the fall Utility Test. Feeling optimistic, I sent in my registration form and entry fee. I had six months to get Zara ready, but I figured I could always withdraw. Committing to the test gave me a solid goal to work towards. Although I had originally been convinced that I would never participate in the Utility Test, by that point, I had been a member of NAVHDA for long enough that it seemed like the logical next step. With Zara showing so much improvement with her retrieving, and having done the water sequences several times, it finally seemed like a feasible goal. I had grown to appreciate the intricacies of NAVHDA's tests and had almost forgotten about entering AKC Field Trials.

At the February training day, I had talked to Steve about my concerns for the test. Since he is a Senior Judge, I knew I could trust his opinion. I told him that I was worried about Zara's steadiness and retrieving. He advised me to concentrate my efforts on retrieving. "Every part of the Utility Test involves retrieving," he said. "And your dog needs to retrieve *to hand*." I thought about the four parts of the test. In the field, Zara would need to retrieve multiple chukar to hand. During the duck drag, she would need to bring a dead duck back to me. After the steady-by-the-blind sequence, there was the water retrieve of another dead duck. And if she found the live duck during the duck search, she would need to bring that back, too.

Steve was right. Not only was the test focused on retrieving, it was focused on retrieving *ducks*. Zara had yet to pick up a duck, dead or alive, so we still had a way to go.

After that training day, I felt like Zara had a solid enough understanding of the e-collar pressure to start using it with the fetch command. I was nervous that I wouldn't be able to do it properly, but I knew I had to.

I put on her e-collar and started with a bumper. I held it out in front of her and said, "Zara, fetch!" As soon as I said the word "fetch," I held down the button for the lowest level of stimulation on the e-collar. As she had with the previous commands, Zara hesitated before taking the bumper in her mouth. I turned off the stimulation as soon as she took it. Then I clicked the clicker and gave her extensive praise and some food. She seemed a little uncertain. We repeated this two more times before moving onto play time.

We did several more sessions like this without much enthusiasm on Zara's part. I still felt like she didn't completely understand the pressure on/pressure off concept. I talked to Emily, and she suggested that instead of using treats to reward Zara, I have her work for her dinner. I liked this idea. I knew that her dinner would be an even more high-value reward.

This was a little trickier since Zara now ate a raw-meat diet. Instead of neatly doling out kibble, I had to make sure the chunks of meat were cut up into small enough pieces to be rewards for our training session. I started this process in April, and it *drastically* improved Zara's mood and her willingness to work. When it was dinnertime, she knew it and was always ready to eat.

I also switched to using the e-collar as a correction instead of initiating the fetch sequence. I knew she had a better understanding of the collar as a punishment for not doing something, since that is how I'd always used it. So, instead of initiating the pressure immediately after saying "fetch," I would only turn it on if she failed to pick up the object. I know this is not how a lot of trainers teach retrieving, but it worked for us.

With the addition of her dinner bowl and the e-collar to enforce the command, Zara's retrieving began to improve. I introduced more dead birds that I thawed from my freezer, including ducks. We worked on long retrieves across my yard, and blind retrieves into piles of brush where she didn't see the bird or object fall. I tried to generalize the retrieving as much as I could. I took dead ducks contained in large plastic bags to the lake when we went hiking and would spend time getting Zara to retrieve them out of the water. I'm sure if people saw us they would have wondered what on earth we were doing, but I didn't care. I had a deadline I was working towards, and I needed to stay on track.

By mid-summer of 2019, I felt like I had finally taught Zara to retrieve. She was enthusiastically picking up any object I directed her to and not dropping them on the way back to me. It had taken me a year to get her solid, but I hadn't been in a hurry. I had time, patience, and a very food-motivated dog. Sometimes, that's all you need to teach a new skill. The process had been long and somewhat tedious, but I found that it had given me a deeper bond with Zara. I was ecstatic that I had been able to teach a five-year-old dog with no desire to pick up dead game to be a good retriever. And my method had worked. I had not had to resort to using the ear pinch or toe hitch, which made me very happy. After going through the process, retrieving became one of Zara's strengths. She never failed to retrieve or dropped a bird in a test after that.

Many months ago, I had been at a NAVHDA training day with Zara, and we were waiting for our turn to do the steady-by-the-blind sequence. I was standing near an older man and his Pudelpointer. No one else was around. He threw a dokken for his dog to retrieve and said, "Fetch!" The Pudelpointer bounded after the dokken and brought it to his owner's side. This was several months into Zara's retrieve training, but she was not yet reliable. For fun, I decided to do the same thing. As the man watched, I threw my own dokken for Zara to retrieve. She ran to it, sniffed it, and walked away. I didn't correct her. I should have known that's how it would go—we were in a new location with lots of distractions around, and I had not begun enforcing the command yet.

I went to pick up the dokken and shrugged. "We're still working on retrieving," I said to the man. To my surprise, he looked at Zara and laughed.

"You can't teach her to retrieve," he said. He said it in such a matter-of-fact way that I was caught off-guard.

"What?" I said, puzzled, returning to him with my dokken.

"You can't teach her to fetch. You're a woman. You don't have the toughness for that."

I laughed, mostly at the absurdity of this statement. He had no idea how hard Zara and I had been working already. He probably didn't realize that she was five, and I had a harder road than most people. I understood that he thought I was not tough enough for traditional force fetch, which I acknowledged was probably true. But that didn't mean the end result couldn't be accomplished by a different means.

"We'll see," I said noncommittally. There was no point in arguing with his logic. Some people may have been offended by his statement, but I was not. Instead, it ignited a fire in me. *I'll show him*, I thought. *Just wait. Just wait until my dog can retrieve better than yours.* I'd seen his dog drop a few birds in the field.

This was the kind of motivation that drove me to work harder. I can get a bit obsessive when I latch onto a goal. Unbeknownst to him, his comment had built me up instead of tearing me down. I thought of him occasionally after I had successfully taught Zara to retrieve, even though I never saw him again. *Guess you were wrong*, I'd think smugly. *Turns out a woman can teach her dog to retrieve.*

As the test was getting closer, I knew that I had to work on Zara's heeling. I had never taught her a proper heel, and even loose-leash walking was still a struggle. When I walked her, she wore a front-clip Freedom harness to cut down on the pulling. It helped, but that was not something she could wear during the Utility Test. Once again, I consulted Emily for assistance on teaching Zara to heel. She suggested using a well-fitting metal prong collar, because it is easy to give corrections using it, which would help Zara learn the proper heel position. A prong collar consists of interlocking metal links that have blunt ends. There's a metal circle where you clip the leash. When the handler gives a quick pull on the leash, the dog feels pressure around their neck. It does not hurt them. Coincidentally, we already owned a prong collar for Zara. We had gotten it a few years prior when we took the Canine Good Citizen class. I had used it during the duration of the class but never felt that it made a drastic difference. Zara still seemed to want to pull the entire time she was wearing it. The instructor encouraged me to give small little yanks with my wrist to stop her from pulling. In retrospect, I think what she needed was more quick jerks and less of the smaller, softer corrections.

I dusted off the prong collar and fitted it to Zara's neck. Unfortunately,

I had used the word "heel" when she was a puppy in an attempt to teach her to walk on a loose leash. In practice, she ended up thinking that heel meant turn around and circle back to me. I wanted to start fresh, so I needed a different word. In reality, I could have used anything, but I didn't want to make a complete fool of myself by commanding, "Zara, potato!" during the NAVHDA test. I chose the word "march" since march is another word for walking forward. It was unusual, but at least it made some sense.

We started off with short sessions in my driveway and the cul-de-sac in front of our house. Zara responded pretty well to the prong collar. Because of the way it's designed, she couldn't lunge forward without putting uncomfortable pressure on her neck. We worked on it each morning, and soon I was using the prong collar on our neighborhood walks, making Zara walk in the heel position instead of slightly ahead of me or wherever she pleased. I was usually also walking Colombo at the same time, but thankfully he was not difficult to leash train. Without a lot of dedicated training, he had developed a natural loose-leash walk. I would heel Zara on my right side and walk Colombo on the left.

Eventually I added the e-collar in addition to the prong collar so I could transition to only using the e-collar. This process went a little smoother than teaching fetch using the e-collar, since I was giving corrections rather than applying pressure and asking for a behavior. I found that heeling was simpler to teach than loose-leash walking. With heeling, there is a defined position where the dog should be. I think this was easier for her to understand than the loose-leash walking. We continued to work on heeling up until the test. After nearly six years of less-than-ideal leash behavior, I knew that it would take time for her to unlearn the bad habits. I wasn't expecting perfection in a short amount of time, but I was seeing improvement.

Chapter 14

Starting to Belong

As summer wore on, we worked on the other parts of the Utility Test, such as the duck search and duck drag. At the NAVHDA training day in July, Zara did a duck search for the first time in 10 months. Instead of going out and refusing to retrieve the duck, she went out into the swamp, found the duck, and trotted back to me. She slowly walked up the bank and sat next to me. I was beaming as I took it from her. "Good girl!" I cried.

Several of the Tarheel Chapter members were watching Zara's duck search. They had seen Zara make progress over the last two years, and they were well-aware that she'd never retrieved ducks before. "I think you've got yourself a bird dog, Terry Ann!" one of them exclaimed after Zara retrieved the duck. I just smiled and nodded. All that retrieving work was paying off.

Zara also had no issues doing the duck drag. I had only tried a duck drag once before teaching her to fetch, because it seemed like a pointless exercise if she wouldn't retrieve. The first duck drag I did after teaching her to fetch went well. She ran straight to the duck, picked it up, and booked it back to me. I was thrilled that all the pieces seemed to be falling into place.

On September 7th, the Tarheel Chapter held the last official training day before the October test. Because bird growers typically don't have mature birds available outside of the October to March hunting preserve season in North Carolina, we had not had access to live birds in six months. This worried me, because steadiness was something that I was still not sure Zara had down.

It was a hot day, and by the time Zara and I got into the field, it was close to 2pm. I had planted several chukar in the field. I was shocked to find that every time the bird was flushed, Zara broke on the gunshot. I felt so frustrated. Looking back, Zara's behavior made sense. She had barely been steady the last time she'd been on live birds in February. Expecting her to be solid after not practicing for six months was silly. But I didn't have enough experience at the time to realize that my expectations were too high.

She also did not do a good job retrieving the dead birds. After I sent her to retrieve a bird, she ended up finding a different live one and going on point. She couldn't find the others at all. I knew that the scenting conditions were bad with the hot weather, but this was still concerning.

During the steady-by-the-blind sequence, she broke on the last gunshot and headed into the water to retrieve the duck before I commanded "fetch." The heeling sequence was also shaky.

At the end of day, I drove home feeling defeated. The test was less than a month away, and it seemed like Zara was far from ready. I texted Emily when I got home with the bad news. *I don't think we're going to be ready for the test! Maybe I should drop down to UPT. I don't want to make a fool of myself.*

UPT, or the Utility Preparatory Test, is a scaled-down version of the Utility test. It's designed as a halfway point between Natural Ability and Utility. However, from what I'd heard, very few people enter the UPT. Although the criteria is not as stringent, once you're training at that level, it usually makes sense just to go for the Utility Test. People had told me that if your dog can get a Prize 1 in UPT, they can earn at least a Prize 3 in UT.

Emily tried to assuage my fears. She reminded me that we had worked really hard and thought we should still try for the Utility level. I wasn't completely convinced. When I saw Chris, I told him what happened with tears in my eyes. He was perplexed at why I was crying. I hadn't been that upset in a long time. Up until that point, I hadn't realized how much the test meant to me. After preparing for it for more than a year, I think I had built it up in my head as the pinnacle of our achievements. And failing the test and making fools of ourselves was not part of the plan.

I ruminated on the day's events for several hours, and after a while,

I knew what I had to do. I would not drop out of the test or change to the Utility Preparatory level. But I would, with less than a month to go, start to e-collar condition Zara to the whoa command. I had never used the e-collar in the field like that before. This would be a last-ditch effort to get her steady, and I didn't know if it was going to work. But at least I had to try.

That week, I went to visit bird dog trainer Grayson Guyer, who was located south of Winston-Salem, NC. Emily had been working with Grayson for the past several months, and she recommended visiting him to get some help with the e-collar conditioning. Grayson showed me how he used leash pressure, a verbal command, and finally, the e-collar to teach a dog to whoa in the presence of a flying bird. He also talked about the importance of being able to stop a dog using whoa while they were running. His method seemed logical to me, although I had a very compressed time frame. However, I knew that Zara had a fairly solid understanding of the verbal "whoa" command, so I hoped that would help the process go a little faster.

I started doing training sessions three times a day—morning, noon, and evening. Over the next several weeks, I was able to get Zara stopping to the whoa command while she was moving fast. Previously, I had only used whoa when she was standing still. I would practice when we were hiking off-leash in the woods or in an open field near my house. I was pleased with her progress and hoped that it would transfer to her field work.

Scott and his wife Kyley decided to hold a few extra training days at their property the two weekends before the test. There were several of us testing at the Utility level who needed a little more practice. I ended up spending both Saturday and Sunday of the two weekends before the test at their place. They were long, hot days. Even though it was late September, it still very much felt like the peak of summer in Lillington. We'd start training at 7am, but the sun would already be brutal by 9am. Over those four days, Zara showed some improvement in her field work. I had the chance to use the e-collar while she was on point to enforce whoa and keep her from moving. It definitely helped, but I also knew that I wouldn't be able to use the e-collar during the test. Most organizations, including NAVHDA and AKC, don't allow handlers to use electronic collars during their tests. In general, Zara seemed to want to do the right thing and please me, but she also had a strong desire for birds. She would typically hold still until the shotgun went off, but then would try to break. After teaching her to retrieve, I found that her desire to get to the shot bird as quickly as possible had escalated.

We also spent a fair amount of time practicing the duck search, but ducks had been hard to come by that summer. The supplier whom Scott and Kyley used to get ducks from in the past was no longer raising them. On that first Saturday, I was sitting on the hillside next to the duck search swamp watching one of the dogs work and talking to Kyley. She was telling me that she sometimes checked Craigslist to see if anyone was selling ducks. "Good idea," I said. We both started searching Craigslist on our phones. I found an ad for mallard ducks that was only 20 minutes from my house. I emailed the woman who posted the ad, and her response came only a few minutes later. She had seven mallard ducks available.

"How many should I get?" I asked Kyley.

"Get them all!" she said. "Someone will use them." I giggled and imagined what Chris would say when I came home with seven ducks. Lucky for me, he had gone to DC for work and was spending the weekend there too.

That evening, I drove to the town of Knightdale to pick up the ducks. On the way there, I asked Emily what I should say if the woman asked what I was going to do with them. "I'm a terrible liar!" I said. "And I don't want to tell her that we're releasing them into a pond and they're probably going to die." If she asked, I decided to tell her that I was picking them up for a friend who lived on a farm and raised birds. This could have been true. Scott and Kyley had a large property with pens for ducks and quail.

Thankfully, the woman who was selling the ducks didn't ask me any questions. She was old, probably in her 80s, and lived at the end of a road that was named for her family. She had a variety of birds: chickens, guinea hens, turkeys, and ducks. She slowly kissed each duck goodbye before placing it carefully into my small dog crate. Inside, I was cringing. I paid her, got the ducks, and got out of there.

The next day, I had to transport the seven ducks to Lillington in the dog crate. Unfortunately, since Chris was out of town, I had to take both Zara and Colombo with me, which meant that the only place the ducks could ride was the passenger seat of my Honda Fit. The other NAVHDA members had warned me that ducks are very messy, but I don't think I realized how bad they could be. I covered the passenger seat with a tarp and put a towel on the floor in an attempt to contain any potential mess. The crate of ducks barely fit, but I got them in. When I drove up to Scott and Kyley's place, Scott saw the ducks riding in the front seat and started laughing hysterically.

"When you first came to NAVHDA two years ago, I bet you never imagined yourself getting so far into this that you'd be having a crate full of ducks ride shotgun in your car," he said.

And it was true. Two years ago I'd been convinced that NAVHDA's testing system was not for me. I had no intention of training Zara to be a duck dog or to retrieve. It didn't seem necessary. But I'd gradually gotten sucked in, and now I was doing things I never thought I'd do. And the truth was, I didn't mind at all.

Unfortunately, the ducks were so accustomed to humans that they kept trying to come back to shore after we released them into the swamp. We had to keep shooing them out, but they didn't want to go. At least the whole adventure gave us something to laugh about.

At the end of those two weekends, I was tired from the early mornings and long days in the sun. But I also felt energized. I had enjoyed training with everyone and spending time working toward a common goal. I finally started to feel like I was a part of the NAVHDA community. For almost two years, I had very much felt like an outsider and that NAVHDA was a family I couldn't break into. At previous training days, when others were standing in groups socializing, I hung back at my car, fussing with my training gear or eating a snack. I'm sure people thought I was uninterested or even snobby, but the truth was, I was just shy. Everyone seemed to be old friends, and I didn't want to barge into conversations uninvited.

But now, after spending so much time with people who were equally as dedicated to training their dogs, I felt like I belonged. Perhaps they had not taken me seriously before, but now that Zara was about to participate in the Utility Test, we had attained a level of legitimacy.

Chapter 15

The Utility Test

I felt wide awake as soon as my alarm went off on Friday, October 4, 2019. Even though it was 4:15am, I got out of bed quickly in the inky darkness. I had loaded up my car the night before; all I needed to do was pack the cooler and get dressed. I put Zara's blaze orange collar on her to match the blaze orange NAVHDA shirt I was wearing. We slipped out of the house, leaving Chris and Colombo asleep in bed.

The closer I got to Rusty Guns Kennel, the more nervous I felt. *What am I doing?* I thought, as I gripped the steering wheel in the predawn light. *I can't do this. I am not qualified for this. These people are going to think I'm a fool. They're going to see right past my NAVHDA T-shirt and Carhartt brush pants and know that I'm not really one of them. Just because I'm wearing the appropriate attire doesn't mean I have what it takes.*

Despite feeling more connected to the other members from all the training we had done the past two weeks, I still felt like an imposter. All kinds of negative thoughts were running through my head. I was not a qualified handler. I had done everything wrong when it came to training Zara; I had started way too late. I had never fired a real shotgun; I certainly didn't own one. Zara was not ready for the test, she was going to break her steadiness, and everyone would think I was foolish for running her.

I didn't want to be seen as a fool.

I tried to reassure myself. *At least you're giving it a try*, I thought forcefully. *How many people can say that? Think of how far you've come! Zara wouldn't even have picked up a chukar a year ago.*

My youthful appearance and compact Honda Fit amongst all the tricked-out pickup trucks didn't help. Even one of the judges noticed it that morning. During the briefing at the beginning of the day, he asked who was a first-time handler. Several of us, including me, raised our hands. His eyes focused on me and my six-year-old dog. He gave us a knowing smile. "Oh, you're running Natural Ability?" he asked.

"Nope, Utility," I said, with a touch of self-deprecation. *They already know I'm a fake*, I worried to myself.

The test started at 7am, and Zara and I were up first in the field. This was the portion I was most worried about, but I was also glad that we were getting it over with in the morning. By some stroke of luck, Zara did a good job in the field. In fact, it was probably the best she'd ever been up until to that point. She did break on the gunshot on the fifth bird, but a quick "whoa" stopped her until I released her again. I knew that NAVHDA's scores are cumulative—meaning that the judges look at the overall picture to determine the score. One misstep like that doesn't automatically disqualify your dog.

At one point during our 30-minute run, Zara locked up, and I hurried to her to flush the bird. I approached from the side, and, as I did, she slowly glanced over at me out of the corner of her eye with an annoyed look that said, "Are you going to flush this bird, or what?" I found it very amusing. I had read about this side-eye behavior but I had never experienced it before. It's a sign of cooperation between the dog and the handler, but still was funny to see in person. After two years of dedicated training, we were becoming a team.

As we walked out of the field and headed towards a small pond where Zara could cool off, I passed by the volunteers and the other handlers who were testing their dogs. "How'd it go?" they asked eagerly.

"It was better than I thought it would be," I said with a smile. After the field work was over, I felt like I could relax. *We had gotten the hard part over with!* We had to wait a while until Zara would perform again. There was field work for several other dogs and the puppy swimming event. NAVHDA tests are long, tiring days that practically go from sunup to sundown.

Finally, at 2pm, it was time for Zara to do the duck search. It was the hottest part of the day, and I checked the weather app on my phone before I took her out of her crate. 97 degrees. *Ugh*, I thought. *It's supposed to be fall.* I opened the crate door and let Zara out. She was shaking with excitement. "Time to go find a duck, baby girl!" I said.

We walked across the field towards the duck search swamp. I tried to keep Zara in a heel, but she was excited and kept trying to get ahead of me. Heeling is not judged prior to duck search, so it didn't really matter. The hot sun beat down on us. I reached the edge of the swamp where the judging team stood. They gave me the instructions, and I positioned Zara on the side of the bank and mounted the shotgun they had given me. I fired one blank shot. Zara didn't move. I paused, and then gave her the command. "Fetch!"

She jumped into the water, and I handed the shotgun back to the judges. All I had to do now was wait and hope that Zara would do the task well. The 10 minutes you spend watching your dog do duck search can feel like the longest 10 minutes of your life, especially if you are willing them with every ounce of your being to go out further and search longer. In training, she had always gone out right away and searched around, even if her range wasn't as extensive as some of the other dogs I watched. However, leading up to the test, I didn't fully understand what the judges were looking for. I didn't realize that in order to earn the highest score, your dog usually has to cover a large portion of the swamp. With years of obedience training and encouragement to stay close to me, Zara was not a dog who would take off in the swamp and not come back. That is generally what you want when it comes to duck search. But going into the test, I thought her duck search was sufficient.

Zara swam out a short distance and sniffed some of the grasses growing in the water. Within a minute or so, she swam back to me and starting running the bank. It seemed like she was trying to pick up the scent of the duck to know where to go, but there was no wind. *No, Zara*, I thought with a groan. I wanted her out of my sight in the water, not on the bank near me.

"Do you want to try throwing a rock?" one of the judges asked. I looked at him and sighed.

"Okay," I said, knowing that my score was dropping by the minute. The judges and I gathered some rocks and threw them into the swamp, trying to lure Zara out. She swam out to the first one, but quickly came back. We tried again, but it didn't work.

"I'm going to resend her," I said. The judges nodded. I called Zara to me and turned her to face the swamp. "Zara, *fetch*!" I commanded. I knew that giving her this second fetch command would likely drop my score one level: from a 4 to a 3, or a 3 to a 2. But it seemed like a necessary step, since she wasn't going out on her own.

Zara paddled out into the water again and searched around the area close to the bank. She never stopped moving, but she also never went very far. Finally, after what seemed like an eternity of torture in the blazing sun, the judges told me to call her back in.

She came to me, and I leashed her up. "Thank you," I said to the judges and walked down the path back to my car. I wasn't sure what my score would be, but it certainly would not be a 4. We needed at least a 2 to pass the test.

The rest of the afternoon went by fairly quickly after that. We had the steady-by-the-blind/water-retrieve sequence and the duck drag. Zara completed those tasks nearly flawlessly. I had to give her a little correction when she tried to move past me as she returned with the duck on the duck drag, but that was it.

With the test over, I felt somewhat relieved. All that was left was to wait for the scores. I chatted nervously with the other handlers. Zara was not the only dog who hadn't lived up to expectations, which made me feel a little better. We had managed to get through the Utility Test with our dignity intact, and she had not done poorly in the field, as I had feared.

I changed into shorts and sat down at a picnic table where the other handlers and volunteers were gathering. I held a cold Gatorade bottle against my cheek. My face had layers of dried sweat and sunscreen. Zara sat at my feet. Everyone was exhausted. It was nearing 6pm, and we had been at Rusty Guns Kennel for 12 hours.

The three judges appeared and positioned themselves at the front of the group. It was time for them to read our scores. I petted Zara on the back and took a deep breath.

"First up was Zara," the Senior Judge began. "Zara is a five-year, 11-month-old Vizsla female, owned and handled by Terry Ann Fernando. Zara and Terry Ann earned the following scores." I could scarcely breathe as everyone's attention was fixed on the judge. The humid air was still.

"Search for a duck: 1. Walking at heel..."

Hot tears rushed to my eyes, and I averted my gaze to my feet, where Zara was lying calmly. I willed myself not to cry. Kyley reached over and squeezed my arm. She knew what the "1" meant. I pressed my lips together, fighting back the tears. *How was that possible?* I knew that Zara had not done a great duck search, but I thought she'd at least gotten a passing score.

The judge continued to read our scores, but I could barely hear him. That one score was more important than all the rest. All the work, time, money, the months and months spent teaching a five-year-old dog to retrieve, and the transformation from pet owner to amateur hunting dog trainer was not enough.

Zara and I had failed the Utility Test.

Finally, the judge concluded his report, saying, "...for a total of 172 points and no prize." Everyone clapped politely, and I could feel the looks of sympathy. I bit my lip to stop the tears.

The judges finished reading everyone else's scores, and Zara was not the only dog who didn't pass the Utility Test. None of the dogs earned a Prize 1, either, which made me feel a little better. Once the judges were done, everyone dispersed to offer congratulations and condolences to each other.

I walked up to the judges and asked them to read my scores again so I could write them down. I had been so thrown by the 1 in duck search that I had hardly heard the other scores. It turned out that Zara had received high enough scores to get a Prize 1 in every other category except for duck search. We were so close.

I was trying to stay composed, but it was difficult, as the other NAVHDA members came up to me to offer a hug or some kind words. Despite the fact that we did not pass, everyone was so supportive.

"Look how far you've come," Scott said. "When you first showed up at that training day two years ago, we never imagined you would have gotten this far. Especially with Zara being an older dog."

"It's true," I laughed, wiping tears from my eyes. "I had no idea what I was getting into."

Mike Neiduski, who was one of the judges that day and the president of the Tarheel Chapter, said, "When you guys came out of the field this morning, I thought, *Hot damn!* She did great in the field."

"I know," I said softly. "She was best she'd ever been today." Mike had watched Zara's transformation from a unsteady dog who refused to retrieve anything to a legitimate hunting dog.

Finally, I thanked everyone and said goodbye. It was almost 7pm, and I had to be back at 6am the next morning to volunteer for Sunday's test, so I wanted to get home. I loaded Zara into her crate and told her she was a good girl. She'd given her best, and I couldn't ask more than that.

Still, I felt sad over the next few days. I had never seriously considered the fact that Zara wouldn't pass the Utility Test. She was completely capable of achieving a Prize 2 or 3, and possibly a Prize 1 on a good day. We had worked *so* hard and overcome so much, it didn't seem possible that our reward was failure. It made me question everything. Maybe I wasn't a good enough trainer. Maybe I should have sent her to a professional. Maybe it was her genetics. She was from field trial lines, not NAVHDA-bred versatile hunting dog lines. Maybe she didn't have what it takes to do a good duck search.

But despite my worries, I kept reminding myself that we had it harder than a lot of other people. I didn't join NAVHDA until Zara was almost four. I didn't have a coop of pigeons and land to train on every day. We had done our best with what we had to work with. That was enough. I could test her again next year.

Chapter 16

Senior Hunter

Two days after the Utility Test, Chris, his father who was visiting from overseas, both dogs, and I packed up the car and headed on a road trip to northern Ohio. We were going to attend the Rhodesian Ridgeback National Specialty, which is a yearly event put on by the Rhodesian Ridgeback Club of the United States (RRCUS). At that event, we would complete a 12-mile endurance run with Colombo, and I would show him in a conformation group of hundreds of dogs. This trip helped take my mind off our failure, and, over the next several weeks, I began to feel better about how Zara had performed. I knew that there was always next year. Our chapter typically held tests in March and October, but I knew that testing Zara in March was not an option. She didn't like cold water, and I had struggled to get her into the water in November and December of the previous year. I knew she wouldn't get in after three months of winter had chilled the water even more.

With the Utility Test out of the way until 2020, I decided to focus on something else. Given all the progress Zara had made in the field, I thought she might be ready for AKC Senior Hunting Tests. Although I had originally been interested in AKC Field Trials before I joined NAVHDA, hunting tests seemed more of a logical step after running Utility. The requirements for hunting tests were more similar to NAVHDA Tests than the rules for field trials. After three years of training, I was excited about continuing to compete with her.

The Senior level is a step up from Junior, which Zara had participated in late 2015 and early 2016. To be honest, though, the jump from Junior to Senior is a big one. In Junior Hunting Tests, dogs must point birds and show general obedience, but that's about it. At the Senior level, dogs have to be steady until the shot and they must retrieve shot birds to within a step or two of the handler. They also must "honor" or "back" another dog's point, although they can be commanded to do so. In AKC Hunting Tests, unlike the NAVHDA Utility Test, dogs are run in braces of two. If one dog goes on point, the other should stop when it sees the first dog. This prevents any competition between the two dogs and also allows for a safe shot. The dogs must stop if they accidentally run into a bird and it flushes, but, again, they can be commanded to do so. This is called a "stop-to-flush." In a real-world hunting scenario, a dog that automatically stops allows for a safe shot of a flushed bird.

By that point, Zara was steady to the fall of the bird, for the most part. Continuing to use the e-collar in the field was helping. She also retrieved to hand. I was a little concerned about her honoring other dogs, but since I would be able to "whoa" her, I figured it would be fine; same with the stop-to-flush. In reality, though, commanding her to stop in the middle of a hunting test turned out to be harder than I anticipated.

I still did not have frequent access to live birds. Yes, I did have the NAVHDA training days once a month, but I was beginning to realize that they were probably not going to be enough. It was difficult to teach concepts like stop-to-flush and honoring without frequent practice. This frustrated me, especially when I was around other people who did have access to live birds or were trainers themselves. They didn't understand what it was like. I also realized that it was probably going to be very difficult to get past the Senior Hunter level without being able to train more frequently. At the Master Hunter level, dogs must stop-to-flush and honor without a command. How would I teach that?

In early December, I signed Zara up for her first Senior Hunting Test. It was a double-double test, so we had the opportunity to run twice in one day. The test was held about an hour north of my house in Raleigh, at a wildlife management area just over the Virginia border. Driving into the WMA early that morning, I was amazed by how spacious and beautiful it was. The grass was tinged with frost. It was in the 30s, but the sun was out. Even though it was chilly, I much preferred the wintry weather to the 97 degrees we'd had in October at the Utility Test.

I parked my car near the other pickup trucks and SUVs in a gravel parking lot. There was a small group of other handlers running their dogs at the Senior and Master levels. After chatting with a few of them,

I was informed that almost all of the dogs had failed the previous day because the grass was so high. The dogs were having difficulty seeing their bracemates to back them. *Great*, I thought. *Just what we need.*

AKC Hunting Tests differ from NAVHDA's Tests in that the field work is not looked at as a whole. In other words, if a dog makes a mistake during the Utility Test, such as breaking on a gunshot, it can keep going. The judges look at the whole picture. So if a dog is perfectly steady on four birds and breaks on the shot on the fifth one, they will likely still get a good and passing steadiness score. Hunting tests don't work like that. If a dog makes a mistake, the judges ask you to pick up the dog immediately, and the test is over. In that sense, I appreciate NAVHDA's level of tolerance. Sometimes good dogs do make small mistakes, and it's nice that they consider the entire performance. AKC Hunting Tests felt like more of a high-pressure environment to me because I was constantly aware that one wrong move would cost us the whole test.

When it was Zara's turn to run, I walked her to the start of the course with my bracemate, a woman and her German Shorthaired Pointer. The two judges were on horseback, bundled up in layers. The one judge asked who Zara's breeder was, and it turned out she knew Jane quite well, as she was also a Vizsla breeder. Having worked with the Conestoga Vizsla Club on their newsletter for several years, I knew the judge by name, but I had never met her. I hoped that Zara would perform well.

The judges told us they were ready, and we released our dogs. Zara and the GSP took off at a gallop, zigzagging down the dirt path that led into the bird field. Typically in hunting tests, the beginning of the course, called the back course, is not planted with many birds. This gives the dogs a chance to burn off some energy. Despite that, I walked quickly to keep an eye on Zara. Since she didn't honor on her own, I knew I would have to be close enough to command her into position if the other dog went on point. So, I was constantly scanning back and forth, keeping an eye on Zara and the GSP. It was nerve-wracking, and my heart was pounding.

After several minutes, we crested the top of a hill into an area with high grass. "We're entering the bird field!" the judges called. I glanced at them and nodded in acknowledgment. Soon after, the GSP went on point at the edge of the field. *Here we go*, I thought.

"Point!" the other handler said, raising her hand.

Zara was searching for birds in another part of the field. "Zara, this way!" I called. She headed toward me and as she got close to the GSP, I gave her the command to stop. "Whoa!" I said. "Whoa!" She stopped several feet back in a good position. I was relieved. I stood next to her and held her collar through the flush and shot of the bird, whispering, "Good girl, whoa." *So far, so good.*

Once the GSP had retrieved the bird, we released our dogs again. Zara headed back into the tall grass, and I followed her. The next thing I knew, a bird flew up in front of her and she slowed down, taking a few steps after it. I wasn't quick enough to realize that this interaction was a stop-to-flush and she should be stopping, not moving toward the bird. I called out whoa, but it was too late.

"Thank you, handler," one the judges said, indicating that I needed to leash up Zara. I tried to hide the expression of bewilderment on my face. Everything had been going so well! I was disappointed as Zara and I walked out of the field back to my car. But I knew that we had a second opportunity to run a little later.

We didn't have to wait too long, since there were only a small number of entries for the Senior and Master levels. On Zara's second run, I walked fast and watched her like a hawk. I was poised to issue a "whoa" command at any second if a bird flushed or the other dog went on point. I was not going to make the same mistake again. We got through the honor okay, and then Zara went on point. I flushed the bird; it flew, but the gunners missed. Zara held through the shot. The bird landed back on the ground. I knew it was still alive. "Should I send her to fetch?" I asked the judges with uncertainty.

"Yes," they said. "She should be able to get it."

I groaned internally. I knew that Zara was going to get confused because the bird was alive. "Fetch!" I said.

She ran to the bird and halted, staring at it. A few seconds passed. I knew I needed to remind her what to do. "Fetch!" I said, feeling like our chances to pass this test were over. I was used to the NAVHDA system, where more than one command typically docks your score. "Zara, fetch!"

After what seemed like an eternity and multiple fetch commands, she finally picked it up and brought it back to me.

After that sequence was over, I was surprised to learn that she passed! Walking back to the parking lot, the gunners informed me that you can give multiple commands at the Senior Hunter level.

"Oh really?" I said. "I was thinking I could only say a command once."

"Oh, no," one of the guys replied. "At the Senior level, you can hack at your dog as much as you want. You have to be quiet during Master, but not Senior."

"Good to know," I said.

A little while later, I picked up Zara's first Senior Hunter ribbon from the clubhouse located a little further down the gravel road on the WMA grounds. I stuck it onto her collar and snapped a photo. Almost four years to the day after she aced her first Junior Hunter test, we had finally gotten to the Senior level. I drove home feeling satisfied.

Chapter 17

Rebuilding the Foundation

At the NAVHDA training day in December, I was talking to another member, Joe, and lamenting the fact that I was having trouble training Zara for Senior Hunting Tests because we didn't have a place to train outside of NAVHDA. Joe suggested that I look into a German Shorthaired Pointer breeder called Cripple Creek Kennels, because he thought they hosted some sort of bird dog club there.

"I'll check it out," I said, thanking him for the tip. After I got home, I Googled Cripple Creek straight away. Joe was right—it looked like they had a club where members could train, and they were located only 45 minutes from my house. I sent an email to the owner and hoped I'd hear back soon.

Cripple Creek's Gun and Bird Dog Club turned out to be exactly what I was looking for. The owner, Jody Bass, lived on the property and owned 35 acres of fields that were cultivated for bird dog trials and training. As a club member, I would have access to a loft of pigeons, electronic bird launchers, an electronic backing dog, quail during hunting season, and an ATV. I could come any time I wanted, as much as I wanted, for $250 a year. It was almost too good to be true. After three-plus years of searching for a place to train, I had finally found the perfect spot. I told Jody I wanted to join immediately after I visited his property in late December.

As 2019 faded into 2020, I started going to Cripple Creek on a weekly basis. I was excited finally to be able to train Zara on things that had not been possible at NAVHDA, such as stop-to-flush. Before finding Cripple Creek, I had worried that we would not be able to get past the Senior Hunter level. Master Hunter and Field Trial Gun Dog stakes were a different ball game altogether—something that would be hard to achieve without regular access to birds. Now, those were finally within my grasp. That fall, I had gotten a small taste of competing with Zara at the upper levels, and I was ready to do more of it.

By this point, I had been around bird dog people long enough that I had a good understanding of what I needed to do to train Zara. My main hangup had been a lack of access to property and birds, especially pigeons. Leading up to the Utility Test in 2019, I had trained Zara to be steady on birds primarily by using a strong whoa command, a leash to restrain her if she tried to break, and later, the e-collar to give corrections when she moved. After seeing how some other trainers worked, I understood that this probably hadn't been the best method. They focused on letting the birds teach the dog, without using a command, unless it was needed.

Once a week, I'd drive the 45 minutes from Raleigh to Spring Hope in the late afternoon, aiming to get to Cripple Creek with an hour or so before the sun set. The air was chilly, and a strong wind blew across the fields, which made the scenting conditions perfect for Zara. After Jody had shown me the ropes, I went into the pigeon coop and collected several pigeons in my bird bag. They were homing pigeons, so, after I was done using them, they would fly back to their coop and could be used again. I picked up the two electronic bird launchers and carried those into the field. Bird launchers are metal contraptions that hold a bird until you press a button on a remote, which releases the bird and launches it into the air. Having control over the flush of the bird like this is very helpful for precise training. I'd find a good spot with some tall grass and put one of the launchers on the ground. I'd pull a pigeon out the bird bag and carefully place it into the launcher, a process that did not hurt the pigeon. I'd close up the launcher and try to remember where I put it, something I was always struggling with.

Then I'd bring Zara out. At first, my number-one goal was to teach her that a flushing bird meant whoa—don't move. She already understood this on some level, but I wanted to reinforce it without having to use any commands. I also wanted to teach her to stop-to-flush. When a bird dog is running in a field, and they accidentally run over a bird without smelling it and cause it to fly, they're supposed to stop automatically as the bird flies off. A stop-to-flush without a command was not something that was required at the NAVHDA Utility level, but it was necessary for Master Hunter and Field Trial Gun Dog stakes.

At first, I attached Zara's collar to a 20-foot check cord, which is essentially a long leash, so I'd have more control of her. I'd let her pull me into the field, and, once we got close to the bird in the launcher, I'd press the button and release the bird. I made sure that the wind was blowing away from her, which meant that she couldn't smell the pigeon. This would simulate the situation where she was running in a test and accidentally caused a bird to fly. If she didn't stop, or tried to take a step as the bird flushed, I'd make her stop with the check cord.

Zara picked up on this quickly. I didn't use the check cord for long, because she soon became very cautious, anticipating that birds could pop up at any time. When she was attached to me with the leash, she'd slowly walk alongside and pause every few seconds, waiting for the flush. This made it hard to tell if she was actually stopping because the pigeon was flushing or if she was stopping prematurely in anticipation.

After a few sessions, I stopped using the check cord and let her run free wearing her electronic collar. Although she was still cautious, she moved more freely than when she was attached to the check cord.

I also wanted to teach her to back other dogs without a command. I started using the club's electronic backing dog. This gadget consisted of a plastic silhouette of a dog that was attached to a metal base. When you pressed a button on the remote, the silhouette would pop up and stand erect like a dog on point. After you were done using it, pressing the button again would make the dog silhouette lay back down.

I positioned the backing dog in the field next to a launcher containing a pigeon so it would look like it was pointing the bird. The tall grass surrounding it would hide the silhouette until Zara got close. I brought Zara out and directed her toward the backing dog. When she got close enough to see it, I watched to see what she would do. She didn't stopped moving, so I launched the pigeon. She stopped, wagging her tail slightly. "Good girl," I said. "Whoa." By then, she was starting to understand that a bird flushing meant she should not move.

I walked over to her and pressed the remote to lay the backing dog down. She jumped when it hit against the metal base. I smiled and gave her a slight bump with my knee. "March," I said, heeling her away from the backing dog and the launcher.

I was surprised at how quickly Zara picked up backing the silhouette. It only took a few repetitions before she would stop and back it without a command. I was pleased and hoped that this would translate to backing real dogs. Unfortunately, that was not the case.

Our next Senior Hunter test was held in mid-January at the Sandhills Pointing Breeds Club, the same venue I had visited three years earlier when I was looking for a place to train. Like our previous test, it was a double-double hunting test, so we had two chances to qualify in one day. I drove down early on Saturday morning. Zara was amped, and I felt nervous. My heart was racing, and my stomach was in knots. I was still new to competing with Zara, and it was hard to control my anxiety. I knew that Zara would do a good job finding birds and retrieving, but I was worried that I wouldn't be able to set her up for the honor properly or that she'd bump a bird and not stop-to-flush. I really wanted her to do well.

By the time it was Zara's turn to run, there were a lot of extra quail in the field. The club had set up the course so that there was a back field where no birds would be shot and a bird field where the gunners were positioned. However, by that point, a lot of birds had moved to the back field, which is where we started. Zara was paired with a female Braque Francais, a rare breed similar in looks to a German Shorthaired Pointer. The judges followed behind on ATVs, which are an alternative to horses. Zara did not seem to be bothered by the sound of the ATVs.

Zara took off when I released her and bounded down the path that had been cut in the field. The other dog followed behind. Zara found a bird quickly in the back field. I walked briskly up to her to flush it. I had my blank pistol at the ready. Since we were not in the bird field, this bird would not be shot. I spotted the quail and kicked it up. Zara perked up to watch it fly but didn't move. "Good girl," I whispered and fired the pistol. At the Senior Hunter level, dogs are allowed to move towards the flush when the shot is fired, but Zara stayed put.

"Okay, now heel her away," the judge said. Even if a dog has broken on the shot, once the handler has called them back and released them again, dogs are not allowed to run in the direction that the bird flew. This is called a "delayed chase." I had practiced this with Zara at the bird dog club, but often she would try to circle back. I stepped closer to her and walked her away from the quail's flight. "March!" I commanded.

Soon after I released her again, the Braque Francais went on point. "Do you want to try to get a back?" the judge asked.

"Yes," I said. For Senior Hunting Tests, honoring in the back field counts as the one honor that is needed. At the Master level, a dog must honor in the bird field—all the way through the flush, shot, and retrieve of the other dog's bird. Honoring in the back field is easier since it doesn't take as long, so I definitely wanted to take advantage of that.

"Zara, this way!" I called. She turned and ran toward me. As she got close to the other dog, I gave her the command to stop. "Whoa!" She slowed down and took a few steps. "Whoa!" She stopped completely and looked at me. I looked at the judge, hoping that this was good enough. I was still trying to get used to giving multiple commands.

"Okay, hold her collar," the judge said. I knelt down next to Zara and grasped her collar. At the Senior level, you hold onto the dog as the other handler works the bird. At the Master level, you cannot restrain the dog while it is honoring.

"Good girl, whoa," I whispered. The other handler flushed the bird and fired his pistol. The Braque broke on the shot, which is allowed at the Senior level. Once the judge gave me the okay, I released Zara.

She ran off, leaping through the tall grass. It was really difficult to see her since she was the same color as the grass. Finally, we entered the bird field. The gunners walked along behind me and the other handler. Zara went on point and handled the sequence well. She was steady through the shot and brought the dead bird right back to me. "Good girl!" I praised her.

"Nice job," one of the gunners said appreciatively.

"Thank you." I was proud of Zara for remaining steady through the shot and retrieving to hand—neither of these were required at the Senior Hunter level. Dogs can break on shot and retrieve within a step or two of the handler.

She found another bird and did well with that one too. After a few more minutes, the judge told us that our 30 minutes was up. "Thank you!" I said, calling Zara to me to leash her up. I was happy that we had had a good run and presumably, another pass.

Sadly, things did not go as well in the afternoon. I had trouble setting Zara up for the honor. This time she was paired with a Gordon Setter, a long-haired black dog with tan on the face and feet. The first time the dog went on point, I commanded her to stop, but the judge said I did it too early, and Zara did not actually see the dog pointing when I gave her the "whoa." They allowed us to continue, and the second time the Gordon went on point, I waited until Zara was actually looking at the other dog, but judges said I waited too late. I felt a bit frustrated, but at least we had gotten one pass that day. I was also pleased with her scores from her first run—she had gotten all 8s out of 10.

I planned to go to another hunting test in Chester, South Carolina, at the beginning of February. It was a two-day test, and I was hopeful that Zara would finish her Senior Hunter title there. Prior to running our first Senior Hunting Test, I had spoken with Melissa Thomas, who is a hunting test judge and a friend of Zara's breeder. I had wanted to get clarification about how the Senior level was judged, since the AKC rule book left some room for interpretation. During our conversation, she mentioned that the Vizsla Club of America was holding its National Gun Dog Championship, a walking field trial, in Virginia in 2020. In order to participate, a dog needed a field trial placement or a Master Hunter title. It was an hour-long event, with dogs running in braces. Dogs had to be steady to the fall of a bird, retrieve, and honor, if the opportunity presented itself.

"If you can get a Master Hunter title on Zara by then, you should consider entering," she said encouragingly.

"Oh, wow, that does sound like a great opportunity," I replied. "I don't know if we can get there this season, though." But instantly, my mind started turning. This was the event that Zara's sire, Bull, had won in 2015 and had placed in multiple times. To think that we might have a chance to participate in such a distinguished event took my breath away. Of course I wanted to go. Could we earn her Master Hunter by the beginning of March? I wasn't sure, but I figured it was worth a shot to try.

I knew it would be tight trying to fit in the five passes needed for

Master Hunter by the time the entries for the championship closed on March 8, 2020. I headed to the hunt test in Chester, hoping that we could earn her Senior Hunter title. I also would use that event to gauge her readiness for Master.

The test was held on Saturday and Sunday, and Zara would run once on both days. She had a good run on Saturday, despite the fact that it was snowing when we started off. Snow was not exactly what I was expecting in South Carolina! She earned a pass on Saturday. Sunday was a different story. I arrived a few hours before it was her time to run and waited around. The waiting was not good for Zara. She knew exactly where we were after being there the previous day and she was *amped* by the time it was her turn.

The hunting test was held on a private farm property with a large hill in the middle of it. The course started at the top of the hill and wound around the valley beneath. Spectators could watch the action from the top of the hill. When I finally released Zara at the start of her run, she flew down the hill so quickly that I had no hope of keeping up with her. I didn't realize it at the time, but this range and independence was reflective of her field trial breeding and would benefit me in later years. Within a few minutes, she'd disappeared in the back of the property near the woods. Although I didn't like to overhandle Zara during tests, I didn't want her out of my sight for too long. I called her numerous times but she did not return. Knowing this was unlike her, I hustled to the woodline, realizing that likely she was on point.

Sure enough, she was pointing a quail. The other handler brought his dog in to honor, and I flushed the bird and shot my blank pistol since we were still on the back course, not near the gunners. Zara stood and watched it fly away, just as I'd trained her. "Good girl," I said, and directed her away from the flying bird. As soon as I'd given her a release command, she was off and running.

We reached the bird field quickly. This is where the wheels began to come off. Although Zara did handle her birds pretty well, I felt out of control handling her, because she really wasn't listening to me as she was zooming around. Once she backed the other dog the first time, I tried to keep her away from him and under control when he was pointing so she wouldn't interfere. It was difficult, because I'd direct her one way and she'd go in the opposite direction. Finally, the run was over, and she had managed to pass. One of the judges had watched her run the previous day, too. When we were finished, he asked how it felt to pass two days in a row.

I laughed. "Well, I think yesterday's run was better than today's," I said.

"Yeah, you're right," he agreed with a knowing smile.

Although I was excited that Zara had completed her Senior Hunter title relatively easily, I knew deep down that we were not ready for Master Hunter. I needed to have her under my control when I was handling her at the highest level, and that was not what just happened. She wasn't showing any inclination to back other dogs on her own accord, and we needed more time to work on an automatic stop-to-flush.

I felt somewhat somber as I drove home to Raleigh. I was disappointed that we wouldn't be able to enter the National Gun Dog Championship, but I tried to comfort myself with the thought that potentially we could try another time. The location moved around the country each year. If it was held out West in 2021, maybe it would return to the East or at least Midwest in 2022. Zara would be eight then, and hopefully she would still be in good shape. Bull was 10 when he'd earned a fourth place ribbon in the NGDC, after all.

Chapter 18

Fixing More Problems

Then, seemingly out of nowhere, the COVID-19 pandemic began to spread across the country. By mid-March 2020, most of the U.S. was locked down in quarantine. Although it was a scary and not very enjoyable time, there was one silver lining for me. The National Gun Dog Championship, which was supposed to be held in late March, was canceled. It would be postponed until March 2021 at the same location in Virginia. I was thrilled. We could certainly be ready in another year! I had access to the bird dog club and hopefully could find other people to help me work on Zara's backing. I set my sights on earning Zara's Master Hunter title in the fall.

Of course, COVID-19 did put a damper on my plans. With the strict lockdown in place, Zara and I didn't visit Cripple Creek for eight weeks from mid-March to early May. It was depressing to be stuck at home and unable to see other people. At least Chris and I had the dogs to distract us. Caring for them meant we had to get outside at least once a day, to go for a walk or a hike. Being outside in fresh air always helps my mood.

During this time, I had acquired a large inflatable exercise peanut, which can be used for canine fitness activities. A dog can be taught to put their paws on the peanut or balance their whole body on the unstable surface, which builds coordination and muscle. One day, I was using it to do some exercises with Zara. After we finished, we went downstairs, and she took a short nap. When she got up a little while later, I noticed she was limping. *Oh no*, I thought. *What happened?* Ever since she was a puppy, Zara has been notoriously injury-prone.

I couldn't identify the exact cause of her limping but eventually concluded it must have been the result of her jumping off the exercise peanut. After a few days without it getting better, I took her to the vet.

She thought it was either a hairline fracture of her toe or a soft-tissue injury. The recommendation was rest and no exercise—even on a leash—for a week. You can imagine how much fun that was with an energetic Vizsla.

Truthfully, this injury could not have come at a better time. In any other year, I would have been upset that we weren't able to train, but given that we were stuck at home anyway, it wasn't the end of the world. It took a few weeks for Zara to fully recover, and afterwards, her one toe joint remained enlarged. The vet thought maybe she had developed a bit of arthritis in that joint after the injury healed. I didn't like it, because it was a visual reminder to me that Zara was not as young as she used to be. She would be turning seven in October. But she didn't seem bothered by it.

By early May, after eight weeks, the North Carolina governor lifted the stay-at-home order. I took this as an opportunity to start going to the Cripple Creek Bird Dog Club again. After all, it was a socially distant activity. Most of the time I was the only one there, or I would see the owner for a few minutes. The rest of the time, I was out in the field alone, except for Zara and a few homing pigeons.

We had started to make some good progress before COVID-19 shut everything down, but we still had a lot of work to do. I had multiple issues I wanted to fix before the Utility Test in October. After the Utility Test, I wanted to run her in Master Hunting Tests. In addition to stop-to-flush, backing, and general steadiness, I wanted to fix her tendency to creep while on point.

She would find a bird, lock up on point, and, after a period of time, would slowly start creeping towards the bird. Needless to say, that was not what she was supposed to be doing. Once a pointing dog smells a bird, they should establish a convincing point and not move until the bird is flushed and the handler releases them (if they have been trained to this level).

I couldn't remember exactly when she started doing this. She had probably done it for several years, since we joined NAVHDA. At training days, we were always using quail or chukar that were planted by hand. Because of that, I didn't have instant control on when they would flush—

THE ACCIDENTAL BIRD DOG

she had to wait while I walked up to her and started kicking around to find the bird. If she went on point far away from me, it would take some time for me to reach her. This delay allowed Zara to start creeping on point without a lot of consequences.

For a long time, I was using a check cord to restrain her and would verbally "whoa" her if she started to move, but it wasn't always precise. By the time we completed NAVHDA's Utility Test in 2019, she was not creeping all the time and would certainly stop if I said "whoa." Introducing the electronic collar also helped. But I didn't want to give any sort of correction. I wanted her to understand that creeping was not an appropriate behavior.

I noticed that she mostly started creeping when the scenting conditions were not ideal. The previous winter, on days when it was clear, crisp, and at least somewhat windy, which was the majority of the time, she would point and hold it. Now that we were training in the summer, it was typically warm and humid without a lot of wind, and I noticed she was creeping more. I assumed she was trying to get closer to the scent when it was not coming at her as strongly.

Now that I was finally able to train on a regular basis with pigeons in launchers, I started going back to teaching Zara that if she took a step after pointing, the bird would go away. So, after she went on point, if she started to creep, I launched the bird immediately.

As the weeks went by, it seemed like I had done a lot of repetitions of this, but she was definitely not 100% there yet. I knew it would take a while to unlearn the habit. When I launched the bird without walking in front of her, she would get what seemed to be a confused expression on her face, like, "Oh, did I make the bird go away?" At least I hoped that's what she was thinking.

Another technique I'd read about was setting up "crosswind finds." You put a pigeon in a launcher, bring your dog out, test the wind to see which way it is going, and then direct your dog so they are running perpendicular to the wind. This way, they should turn their head as soon as they pass through the scent cone of the bird. The scent cone is the area surrounding the bird in which a bird dog can smell their odor. If they don't establish point immediately, you launch the bird.

While this sounded great in theory, I found it difficult to execute in practice. You definitely need a strong wind, and you have to be able to control the path of your dog very well. It was probably easier to do this on a check cord, but I didn't like to have Zara on a check cord at our training field. Whenever I did that, she slowly stalked along next to me, because she knew something was about to happen. Then it was hard to tell if she was pointing or just stopped, because she thought a pigeon was about to pop up.

I also wanted to fix her tendency to parade around with a dead bird before bringing it right to me. When I'd taught her to fetch over a year ago, I'd tried to be consistent about having her come directly to my right side and sit next to me before I would take the object away. This type of "presentation" looks really nice when the dog does it in the field and is rewarded in the NAVHDA system. However, I noticed that Zara started to behave differently with birds when we were not training at home. In my yard, when I was working on retrieves with her, she would go get the object and bring it straight back to me without any issues. But during training days, she would sometimes run to the bird, pick it up, and start going in the opposite direction. Or she would pick it up, come towards me, but then veer around me, like she was taking a victory lap with the bird.

I tried to figure out the cause of this. Was she playing keep away? Did she know that I typically didn't have treats when we were away from home so she was resistant to bringing the bird back? Or was she excited about other people being around and wanted to show them her prize?

I went back to the basics and starting working on retrieving drills with her at home using a place board. A place board is typically a small platform that is raised several inches off of the ground. It gives a dog a defined spot to come to or stay on. During the lockdown, I made my own place boards using pieces of wood and cheap door mats from the Dollar Store that I stapled on top to provide traction. I would set the place board directly next to my right side and put Zara in position next to me. I would give her a "whoa" command, throw a bumper or dead bird, and tell her to fetch. As she returned to me, she had a clear spot to go to—the place board. I hoped by reinforcing this spot, it would translate to when she was in the field without the board.

I also tried letting her hold onto the object for a little while before I took it away from her. Once she returned to me and was holding it, instead of asking her to give it to me immediately, I would give her a heel command start walking around, letting her carry it. Eventually, I would stop and then ask for it.

Although I was hesitant to use the e-collar to correct this behavior, I tried that as well. If she picked up the object and started veering away from me, I would give her a mild collar correction along with a verbal "ah-ah!" This was something I could use in the field more readily.

However, the main thing we needed to work on in the summer of 2020 was duck search. Although Zara and I had worked on duck search the previous summer, I didn't have a real plan, and, to be honest, I didn't fully understand what the dog had to do in order to earn the highest score. Although Zara did have some natural desire to go into the water and look for ducks, she was not the type of dog who dragged their owner to the shore and bounded into the swamp as soon as they were released, gung ho on finding a duck, no matter what.

I had learned that many trainers advise teaching duck search before any steadiness work is introduced. Sometimes this is referred to as "go before whoa." It's often easier to reel in a dog's tendency to swim off and not come back than it is to try to push a dog out who has undergone a lot of steadiness work and has been taught to stay close to their owner. Unfortunately, I had already done years of steadiness work with Zara before we started serious duck search training. But this was not the first time we had to deal with an obstacle, so I was not discouraged.

One of the guys in my NAVHDA chapter had gained access to a property east of Raleigh with an ideal duck search swamp. He invited a few other members and me to train there in late May. Since Zara had not done a duck search in more than six months, I wanted to take it slow. Instead of having someone place the duck in the middle of the swamp, I had one of the guys we were training with drag the duck out from the shore to leave a bit of a scent trail. This worked well. I brought her up to the shore and sent her to find the duck. She successfully followed the scent and located the duck. She retrieved it back to me, and then went out again on her own accord. Practicing resending your dog during duck search is important, because you will usually have to resend the dog without another shot if they find the duck quickly during the Utility Test.

The second time we practiced, I went to visit Emily and Grayson at the farm where they trained in Winston-Salem. This time, Grayson wore waders and walked out into the swamp. He placed a duck about 50 yards out, but he did not drag it through the water first. Again, Zara had a fairly easy time locating the duck, but I believe she was able to follow his scent from the shore, since she followed his exact path.

In mid-June, we did our third duck search of the season. This time, I wanted to see what Zara would do without any scent from the send-off point. I had a friend, Wes, with whom we were training, paddle out away from shore in a boat and place the duck about 50 yards out. Zara struggled with this. I sent her, and she went out, obviously searching for the scent with her nose. After searching the area near the shore, she seemed unwilling to go out any farther. I asked Wes to go out in the open area of the pond in the boat and encourage Zara to come with him. He did so, and Zara followed, eventually picking up on the scent of the duck and bringing it back. She went out again and found the other duck, again with a little bit of help from Wes.

In retrospect, I was expecting too much from Zara during this third duck search. It would have been beneficial for us to continue dragging ducks through the water to provide scent trails so I could have solidified her understanding of what I wanted her to do. Once she had a handle on this, I could have weaned her off the scent trails.

We continued to work on duck search for the rest of the summer. I definitely saw improvement over the previous year. If Zara caught scent of the duck, she would follow it and expand her search. But often she needed some encouragement to get out there. If someone was in a kayak helping me, Zara would gladly swim along with them to find the duck. Using electronic launchers helped as well. We would put a duck in a large launcher and set up the launcher (that had been rigged to a circular flotation ring) in the swamp. Once Zara was near the launcher, we'd launch the duck to get her attention and encourage her to go farther out. I probably saw her do a few duck searches that were worth a score of "4"—the score needed to get a Utility Prize 1. But she was not consistent.

Despite this uncertainty, I had my sights set on earning a Prize 1.

Given that Zara had been at that level for everything except for duck search last year, I thought it would be achievable. I had signed up for the Tarheel Chapter's fall test again, which would be held in early October 2020, as long as COVID didn't spiral out of control. But I didn't want to put all my expectations on this one test. I had seen all too easily last year how a test day could end in disappointment. I decided to sign up for a second test to increase our chances of getting a Prize 1 and qualifying for the Invitational. In a normal year, it's not uncommon for handlers to sign up for multiple Utility Tests. But with COVID canceling all of the late-spring and early-summer tests, there was a lack of test spots for the fall. I managed to find a spot for late September—the weekend before we'd test at Tarheel. This test was put on by the Budds Creek Chapter, a brand-new chapter based in southern Maryland. Given the lack of test openings, I felt slightly guilty about potentially taking a spot from someone else. However, Zara was almost seven. We didn't have the luxury of time that many others did. I threw myself into training, convinced that these two opportunities would give us a good chance of earning a Prize 1.

In August, I finally had the chance to test Zara's steadiness on quail and chukar. Because of the lack of pen-raised birds over the summer, she hadn't seen a live quail or chukar since February, six months ago. Of course, unlike the previous summer, we had been working with pigeons weekly, so I wasn't too worried. I knew that a shotgun blast and the subsequent fall of a bird would be more stimulating than a pigeon flying away, but I figured she could handle the pressure.

That spring, a new NAVHDA chapter had been formed, centered around the Winston-Salem/Charlotte area of the state. Since it was fairly close to the Tarheel Chapter, there was a lot of overlap in membership. I decided to attend their August training day, since the chapter had access to live birds. I pre-ordered my three chukar and drove to Randleman, NC early one Saturday.

The training day was held at a hunting preserve. The fields had grown up so much over the summer that portions of the grass were as tall as I was! There were other shorter sections, thank goodness, but it was thick and wet. Wet birds typically don't fly very well. We ended up putting the birds in electronic launchers in order to keep them dry and get them to fly. Despite these challenges, when it was Zara's turn in the field, not only was she steady through the gunshot, she managed to retrieve a bird in such thick cover that we were all cheering when she finally brought it out. I was pleased.

I also drove to Maryland twice that summer to train with the Budds Creek Chapter. I mainly wanted to expose Zara to their duck search water. Their swamp was different than the one at Rusty Guns Kennel. It was a small pond enclosed in tall reeds. About 50-to-60 yards out, there was a small opening that went to another swamp, with lily pads floating on the surface.

The first time I went, Zara struggled with the duck search. She swam out partway but then headed back. I had to get another member to hide in the reeds and make quacking noises before she would go out far enough to find the duck. Given that she was the first dog in the swamp that morning, there was no scent trail in the water from the other dogs bringing back ducks. Eventually she found the duck and brought it back. The second time we went, in September, she did one of her best duck searches. As soon as I released her, she swam straight across the water towards the opening to the back swamp. She thoroughly searched the reeds and went into the further swamp. She easily was out there for more than 10 minutes, but she still had not located the live duck. Training with live ducks, even ones that had had their flight feathers pulled, can be tricky. You can't always predict where they will go. This is when I made a mistake I would regret later. I should have had someone throw a dead duck in the vicinity so that she could get a reward for her effort. But I hadn't brought my own duck (since I was traveling), and, given that it was not my chapter, I felt uncomfortable asking to use someone else's duck. I called her back in and praised her, but I broke a cardinal rule of duck search training: you should always have the dog succeed. It's okay if they don't find a duck on test day, but, ideally, they should find one every time you are training. This teaches them that searching pays off.

Summer was coming to an end, and I was counting down the days to the Utility Test. At our last Tarheel training day before the test, I took Zara out in the field and, unlike a year ago, she was perfectly steady on the four chukar I planted for her. She didn't creep, she didn't break on the shot, and she retrieved them back to me without too much parading around. I was happy and figured I'd leave it at that. Better to end on a high note than have a bad experience before the test.

The Budds Creek Test was held on the last weekend in September. I was feeling pretty confident going into the test. However, the weather forecast was calling for rain, and the grass was very wet when we arrived early that morning. At all the tests I had been to, field work was always done first, to get it over with before the heat of the day. But with the rain and wet fields, the judges decided to do field work last. Duck search would be first. I started worrying about the water temperature, because I knew that Zara didn't like cold water. It was a cool morning compared to the preceding months, with temperatures in the low 60s. But there was nothing I could do about the weather.

Zara was third in the running order. When it was our turn, I brought her up to the edge of the water, positioned her in a sit, and fired the blank shot. I paused and said, "Fetch!" Zara hesitated. I groaned internally. *Not again!* I thought. I was sure it was because of the cool water temperature. Zara ran up and down the bank for a minute and then finally got in the water and swam out. *Thank goodness*, I thought. She got about halfway across the water and then headed to the reeds on the right side. She searched around and then came back after a few minutes. She paused at the shoreline. I did not make eye contact. She headed over to the left side of the swamp, looking in the grasses close to shore. After several minutes, the judge requested that I call her back. As I leashed her up and walked back to my car, I felt disappointed. There was no way that performance would earn a 4. But at least we still had another test.

She did well at the steady-by-the-blind and duck drag. We finally got to do the field work in the afternoon. Zara was hyped by this point, and she took off as soon as I released her. She ended up finding all five chukar in the first 20 minutes, and then we had to wander around in circles in the field to burn the remaining 10 minutes. While her steadiness was good, her retrieves were a bit sloppy. Apparently my efforts to improve her retrieve that summer had not paid off. I had to give her multiple commands to come to me with the birds because she was trying to parade with them.

At the end of the day, I knew that Zara had not gotten a Prize 1. But, at least this time, I was sure that she had passed. The judges read the scores and Zara ended up with a 2 in duck search and a 2 in retrieve of the shot birds in the field. She did well on everything else. However, the 2 in duck search knocked her to a Prize 3. It was disappointing, especially since she had done such a great duck search the previous weekend. But I tried not to get too caught up in the results, because we still had one more shot at the Utility Test.

I drove home to North Carolina the next day and spent the following week doing retrieving drills with Zara. One of the other participants in the test had given me a suggestion to improve Zara's desire to parade with the bird. I had always encouraged her to come to my right side and sit, presenting me with the bird. This polished ending is what most people strive for in NAVHDA. Although most people have the dog come to their left side, I trained Zara to come to my right side since that was the side I heeled her on. The woman suggested that it might be better to have Zara come directly to me instead of swinging around to the side. She'd had a similar issue with her dog, and she felt that coming to the front was easier.

I liked her suggestion and decided to try it. When practicing at home, I put the place board directly in front of me instead of to the side. I hoped that this would translate to the field.

Saturday, October 3, 2020 was the date of the Tarheel NAVHDA Utility Test and also my five-year wedding anniversary. For the first time, Chris would drive down to watch the end of the test and hear the scores. Unlike the previous year, the weather was not that hot: the high was 72, the low 51. It would be pretty much perfect for an early fall test, although I was worried that the duck search water would be a bit cold for Zara. It had also been chilly leading up to the test, so the water temperature was lower than in 2019.

I felt less nervous going into the field portion of the test than I had the previous year, although her sloppy retrieving at the Budds Creek Test was still on my mind. Unfortunately, the birds were not cooperating that day. After Zara went on point, three out of the five planted birds flushed before I could get close enough to do it myself. Zara took several steps on the flush, which is not ideal. We had practiced this scenario with pigeons in launchers many times that summer, where I would be standing far away from the bird when I launched it. But perhaps the smell of chukar, and the bird getting up on its own without being flung out of a launcher, was too much.

The gunners didn't shoot any of those birds, since they were not in a safe position. Zara had an opportunity for a retrieve on the last two chukar she pointed, but she got antsy when the shot went off. Since I thought she was going to break, I gave her a stern "whoa." Ideally, you shouldn't be giving any commands during the flushing sequence. This can dock your steadiness score. The one positive was that her retrieves were a little better than they had been the previous week.

As we walked out of the field, my fellow NAVHDA members asked eagerly, "How did it go?" From where they were sitting, it was difficult to see what had happened.

"It could have gone better," I said with a tight smile.

I walked back to my car to put Zara in her crate. I called Chris and broke down crying. Zara had done better in 2019, which was hard to wrap my head around. How was it possible that she'd done *worse* after another whole year of training? It already seemed like our chance at a Prize 1 was gone. Chris reminded me that I never had it easy, with Zara being four years old when I joined NAVHDA. I knew he was right, but I still felt upset.

"It'll be easier with the next Vizsla, since you'll be able to train that one from the beginning," he said.

I smiled. "Wait, you're going to let me get another Vizsla?" I asked. Chris had been claiming that he didn't want another Vizsla because they had too much energy. I was convinced that I just needed to wear him down over time. Maybe my job would be easier than I thought.

"Not for a long time," he said.

"Haha, okay." Chris told me he was planning to drive down to the test site later and told me not to worry. I hung up and pulled myself together. We had a few hours to wait before it was Zara's turn at duck search.

I knew duck search was her weakness, and it was the event I'd been most worried about. But I was kicking myself as soon as I released her towards the water during the test. She hesitated along the shore, dipping her toes in and whining. I knew from the crying that she wanted to go in, *knew* she should go in, but she was resisting because of the chilly water. She ran the bank for what felt like forever as I ignored her and stared intensely into the swamp, trying to will her in. *I should have gotten her wet before we came up here!* I thought to myself with instant regret. *How did I not think of that?!* I knew that she didn't like cold water and I was worried that this exact situation would happen. But I didn't think through any strategies to help her. Tears welled up in my eyes as I watched our chance at Prize 1 slip away.

"Do you want to give her another command?" the judge asked. I squeezed back tears, as flashbacks from Zara's reluctant duck search at the previous year's test came to my mind.

"Zara, come," I said. She walked over to me and I held her collar. "FETCH!" I screamed. I released her collar and she went into the water and started swimming out to the middle of the swamp. I felt a small sense of relief.

"Are you breathing yet?" the judge whispered to me in a joking manner.

I just shook my head without looking at him, my lips pressed together, willing the tears back. I didn't want him to see me cry. He didn't know how much this meant to me.

Zara swam further out and searched left and right. I cheered her on in my head, willing her to keep going. She headed towards where the duck had been thrown but did not go far enough to find it. She started heading back towards me and I turned my head to the side, pretending to be looking at something interesting on the left side of the swamp. *Don't come back, don't come back*, I shouted at her in my head. She turned into the channel of water surrounding the vegetation and headed towards the woods. *Okay, good*, I thought. *Go on, baby, go!*

The minutes felt like hours, and I had no idea how long she'd been out there. I refused to look at my phone to check the time, lest she sense my movement and think it was a command to come back. Eventually, she did come back to the shore, shook, and then headed back out again. After she'd gotten about 15 yards into the swamp, the judges told me to call her back. "Okay," I said. "Zara, come!" She turned towards me and swam back.

I was sure that her performance was not worthy of a 4. A second command typically drops your score down one level, and I knew her hesitation in the beginning was not a good look. We still had to get through the duck drag and steady-by-the-blind sequence, so I headed back to my car and tried to focus. Thankfully, those two events were Zara's strongest, and she completed both of them without any issues.

At the end of the day, when the judges read the scores, Zara and I received a Prize 2. She had gotten a 3 in duck search and a 2 in steadiness in the field. Even if she had done a great duck search, she still wouldn't have gotten a Prize 1.

Like the previous year, I was overcome with emotion after I heard her score. Yes, we had passed, but it was not the result I had been hoping for. The COVID-19 pandemic made the congratulations and condolences between chapter members awkward, and I only wanted to go home after the long day.

Chapter 19

Feeling like a Failure

I felt empty inside. Zara had passed the Utility Test, twice now, but it felt like nothing. It only felt like failure. I remembered how I had felt when she didn't pass in 2019 and how upset I'd been then. Even though she'd actually passed with a Prize 2, I was more upset than I had been when she'd failed. Last year, we had just barely made it over the hump of training—she was somewhat steady to shot, had just learned to heel, and was not doing extensive duck searches consistently. I'd known that she was capable of passing, but I probably would have been happy with any prize.

This time was different. I had spent another full *year* fine-tuning her training. After joining Cripple Creek, we had worked on steadiness, creeping, and stop-to-flush for nine months. She had done multiple duck searches over the summer. I had worked on heeling weekly and tried in vain to fix her retrieving issue of parading with freshly shot birds. It had been a long year, with months of anticipation building up to this test. I was so hopeful this time around, not just for a pass, but a Prize 1. I knew she could do it, and I wanted it—*bad*. I wanted to prove to myself, and everyone else, that we had finally made it. A Prize 1 would do that. A Prize 1 would prove that despite the fact that Zara had a late start, and I was a newbie who no idea what I was doing, that we were not imposters any more, that doing the impossible *was* possible, that you didn't have to be a professional trainer with a dog trained from birth on birds, and that you could do it with a special dog and a special bond.

I also really wanted to go to the Invitational. A Prize 1 Utility dog was one thing, but a shot at a Versatile Champion title was on another level altogether. How amazing would it be to be surrounded by the best NAVHDA dogs in the country? To be on their level? That summer, I had been training with others who had their sights set on the Invitational as well, and I think I got swept up in their high expectations. At this point, I didn't fully understand that NAVHDA tests are never a guarantee at any level. Because there are so many different parts of the test, it can be difficult to get everything to line up on the same day, even for the most well-prepared dog and handler. When I'd first joined NAVHDA in 2017, I'd had no interest in participating in any of these tests. Now, succeeding in them was all I wanted.

But it was not to be, and that was a hard pill to swallow. Although NAVHDA allows you to test your dog at the Utility level as many times as you want, I was leaning towards not testing her again. She was about to turn seven years old. A Utility Prize 1 in 2021 would mean that by the time we got to the Invitational in 2022, she'd be nearly nine. While that certainly wasn't a disqualification, I wanted to be realistic. *Would she still be in top form in two years?* I didn't know.

I also wasn't sure I wanted to deal with another summer of trying to coordinate opportunities for her to do duck search. There was a lot of work involved in setting up duck search training, and it was certainly something we'd need to work on again.

I was disappointed, disappointed in the outcome, disappointed that we didn't qualify for the Invitational, but most of all, disappointed in myself. I was not, however, disappointed in Zara.

Her shortcomings, I knew, were the direct result of my training, or lack thereof. After the test, I played the day's events over and over in my mind. *I should have done more*, I thought. *I should have established more of a consistent training plan. We should have practiced more on chukar instead of pigeons. Why didn't I get her wet before she had to go into the chilly duck search water?* Thoughts like this went on and on, spiraling in my head.

I kept thinking that I had let her down. She was not reaching her full potential because I was holding her back. In someone else's hands, I lamented, she could have been a great bird dog—a fantastic competitor, just like her sire, winning National Field Trial Championships and making it look easy. She had shown so much promise as a young dog at her first hunting tests, and I worried that I had squandered it, spending years stumbling along, trying to figure out how to train her myself.

But in someone else's hands, she may have been nothing at all. She may have never been given the opportunity to hunt, or she may have faltered under someone else's harsh techniques. After all, it was *my* hands that had taken a four-year-old house dog and guided her to become a versatile hunter, capable of finding and retrieving birds, independently searching for ducks, and attaining a level of obedience I only dreamed about when she was a puppy.

Still, the Prize 2 stung. That Prize 2, something I would have been thrilled about just a year ago, wasn't enough. I felt like it exposed me as a novice trainer, even though, to be frank, I *was* a novice trainer. *Other people could earn Prize 1s with their dogs, why couldn't I?* I thought. Of course, many of them had started with young dogs, without any baggage or bad habits to trip them up. I'd started with a four-year-old Vizsla who didn't retrieve and had had zero exposure to ducks. Three years later, the fact that we'd gotten any prize at all was nothing short of a miracle.

I realized that somewhere along the way, I had gotten caught up in the accolades, instead of focusing on the journey. When I first decided to dive into the bird dog world to train Zara to an advanced level, my sole goal was to be able to compete with her—not win—just compete. I had achieved that goal, but now I found that being in the ring was not enough. I wanted the spoils, too, Prize-1-level spoils.

Of course, the pressure was all self-imposed. As a puppy, Zara was sold to my husband and me as a pet, with no performance expectations. Our breeder didn't even require her to earn a Canine Good Citizen title. She just wanted her to be loved and cared for. We had certainly accomplished that. Zara was more than loved; she was adored, and she lived a life that her Vizsla ancestors, owned by Hungarian royalty, would have envied.

But as I became more and more involved in training Zara to be a finished bird dog, I felt a constant sense of having to prove myself. I was not a typical hunting dog owner, being young, female, and not having grown up hunting. I could feel the skepticism directed my way as I pulled up to bird dog events in my tiny hatchback Honda Fit, surrounded by a sea of pickup trucks. Thankfully, Zara was my saving grace. Zara was the one with the talent, and the onlookers only had to watch her to understand why we were there. I felt that a NAVHDA Utility Prize 1 would finally prove, once and for all, that we did belong.

However, the amount of congratulations and support I received from the bird dog community when Zara earned a Prize 2, and even when she'd failed the year prior, proved that I was wrong. We had actually belonged the whole time. People may have been skeptical at first, but they were inspired by us. Me, a novice with a strong case of imposter syndrome, and Zara, a pampered middle-aged Vizsla who had shown no hunting instincts as a puppy. I hadn't realized it initially, but we were blazing a trail for others like us, making space to diversify the bird dog world just a little bit.

And the good news was that Zara did not feel my disappointment. She didn't know that she'd gotten a Prize 2. The feeling that I had disappointed her was all in my head. She didn't care. She didn't know what a test was, and she didn't care about the outcome. She just knew that she was outside having fun with me, running around and finding birds. Recognizing that made my feelings of disappointment start to dissipate.

I also started thinking about how different it would be with my next dog. If that dog was exposed to birds at eight weeks or even earlier, encouraged to carry things around as a puppy, tried duck search at a young age, plus the fact that I'd have a better idea of what I was doing, then earning a UT Prize 1 and a shot at the Invitational would probably be a lot easier.

But would it mean as much? Would it be more exhilarating? More gratifying? Probably not. I doubted any future bird dog would ever be as special as my "accidental" bird dog.

Chapter 20

Woodcock Hunting

In December 2019, Zara and I went hunting for the first time. I know that many people get bird dogs because they want to hunt wild birds with them, and the training and testing is all an effort to prepare them for that or a way to occupy them in the off-season. Not for me. I had never even considered hunting with Zara. My sole focus was on tests and competitions with birds that had been raised by humans. I didn't really know anyone who hunted or who might invite me on a hunting excursion. Yes, there were people in NAVHDA who did, but at that point, wild bird hunting seemed like another world altogether. I know this might sound crazy to people who hunt regularly, but I didn't really see the value of wild birds. *Pen-raised birds were good enough, weren't they?*

But in late December, my friend Emily invited me to go woodcock hunting, and I thought it would be fun to try. Woodcock are small, migratory birds with long beaks that feed primarily on earthworms. They can be found along streams and creek bottoms in thick cover. They migrate from the northern U.S. to the southern states every winter.

We met up at a national forest a few days before Christmas. It was rainy and cold. I didn't own a shotgun, but Emily carried hers. She brought Blitz, her GSP, who had been around woodcock several times before. I had heard that woodcock smell somewhat different from other birds, because their diet is protein-based instead of fruit- and seed-based. I wasn't entirely sure that Zara would be able to sniff out a woodcock, but I hoped that Blitz would show her the way.

We drove to a deserted parking area and unloaded the dogs. It was lightly raining. Zara seemed excited to be in the woods, despite the weather. I had on flannel-lined brush pants, knee-high rain boots, and a winter coat that would be soaked by the time we were finished.

We released the dogs and started walking along a creek. Zara didn't seem to know what we were looking for, but Blitz was hunting away. We walked around for a few hours, cutting through briars and small trees, trying to follow the creek bottoms. Neither dog had shown any indication that there were birds in the area.

We were just about ready to go home when we crossed a small stream and walked through a patch of dense undergrowth. Woodcock are notorious for hiding in thick cover, and, since it was raining, this was even more likely. All of a sudden, Blitz went on point. I tried to get Zara over to the area so she could smell the woodcock, too. Emily moved in to flush the bird, and a group of several woodcock erupted from the ground, whistling as they flew up. We cried out in surprise, and Emily fired a few shots. There must have been four or five birds in that one area.

"Whoa, that was crazy!" I exclaimed as we made our way out of the brush.

"Did you get a chance to see any on the ground?" Emily asked.

"No," I said. "I wasn't able to get close enough."

We continued on, heading back towards the car. When we were almost at the road, Blitz went on point again on the other side of the stream. I gave Zara a "whoa" command. Again, Emily moved in and called that she could see the woodcock sitting on the ground. She motioned for me to come up. I slipped over to where she was and saw the large eye of the bird staring back at me.

"Aw, it's so cute!" I exclaimed. The woodcock was plump, with beautiful brown feathers and an eye that was watching my every move. As I stepped back, it flushed, flying across the road. Emily didn't have a chance to shoot. Blitz and Zara perked up, but remained in place.

"Wow, I can't believe we saw another one," Emily said. "That was what, five or six total?"

We released the dogs and headed back to the car. We were soaking wet and cold, but it had been worthwhile. Flushing five woodcock on public land in North Carolina would be considered a pretty good day in most upland hunters' books. This area of the country is not known for holding a lot of wild birds. I wasn't sure if Zara had gotten a chance to smell the woodcock, but I hoped that she was starting to learn.

After this first experience, I became more interested in hunting. I listened to hunting podcasts, such as the *Project Upland Podcast*, and read articles about hunting. I especially liked Project Upland's website content because they featured people of color, women, and millennials. Both their website and magazine were designed well, which I appreciated as a graphic designer. Hunting, something I'd always looked down upon, began almost to seem cool.

Also, after many years of being uncomfortable around guns, I had finally reached the point where being around shotguns did not bother me. This was due to the numerous NAVHDA training days I'd attended, where I'd watched the other members carry their break-open shotguns in the field. I saw that guns could be handled in a safe manner, and I liked the style of these break-open guns—it was a physical sign that they could not be discharged.

I was interested in buying a shotgun for myself, but I didn't know where to start. I researched on the internet and also talked with fellow NAVHDA members, Wight and Steve Greger. Wight let me try out her two guns. She explained what to look for when buying a shotgun and advised that I visit stores alone, lest the employees try to sell the gun to my husband instead of myself.

I ended up visiting five stores in the Raleigh area, looking for a reasonably priced break-open 20- or 28-gauge over-under shotgun. The selection was limited, and I soon realized that these guns were designed for the average-sized man, not a woman. I tried multiple shotguns, where I couldn't see over the barrel to the bead at the end. According to my research, this was due to the fact that women have longer necks than men. I needed a gun with a raised comb, or a "Monte Carlo" style comb. Unfortunately, this style of shotgun was not something the stores carried, and I couldn't order one to try without paying for it first, which was not something I wanted to do.

I eventually found a $25 comb-raising kit on Amazon.com, which consisted of a foam pad that you could place under a stretchy sleeve that went over the stock of the gun. This solution allowed me to see over the top of the gun. I finally settled on an entry-level CZ Drake 20-gauge shotgun at a local gun store, and I took it home the Monday after Zara's Utility Test in 2020. This purchase cheered me up slightly. I was looking forward to doing something besides NAVHDA training for the next few months.

In November, the quail and woodcock season opened in Virginia. Given that I lived only about an hour from the Virginia border, I bought a Virginia hunting license and headed to a public wildlife management area hoping to find some birds. Although I enjoyed watching Zara work, we did not find any birds on our first trip. I wasn't entirely sure that Zara knew how woodcock smelled. I didn't think she had gotten close enough to those that Blitz found the previous year to really understand what she was looking for.

Thankfully, that soon changed. I met up with Emily a few weeks later at a WMA in central NC. It was not hunting season yet, so we didn't carry our guns. Zara and Blitz ran ahead of us, having a blast. After an hour or so, we headed back towards the cars. Blitz was to the left of us, in a stand of thick pine trees. Suddenly, Emily stopped and looked at the remote to Blitz's tracking collar. A tracking collar is similar to an electronic collar, except it includes GPS technology so you can see how far away your dog is and in what direction. "Blitz is on point!" she exclaimed. We stopped walking and turned towards the pines.

"Zara, come!" I called. If there was a woodcock, I wanted to get her into the vicinity if possible. We started pushing aside branches to reach Blitz. The pine needles scratched my coat as I struggled to move through them.

"There she is!" Emily whispered. Blitz was standing solid off to my left. Zara came in behind me and stopped suddenly. I couldn't tell if she stopped because she was backing Blitz or if she smelled the woodcock. Her stance was not as rigid as it normally was when she was on point. We waited a few seconds and suddenly a woodcock rose from the ground about six feet in front of Zara. She took a few hesitant steps forward and then took off, chasing it.

"Good girl!" I cried. Emily released Blitz, and we made our way out of the woods. Zara eventually came back. I was thrilled that she had seen, and likely smelled a woodcock.

This encounter proved to be the catalyst to Zara's first hunting season. The next time I went woodcock hunting with her, we saw a few birds. Although she did not point any, she started pointing the areas where they had just been. I could assume this because I saw them land and fly off. Within a few visits to a nearby WMA, my seven-year-old dog who'd never hunted wild birds was reliably finding and pointing woodcock. It was thrilling to watch. Even though North Carolina is not known as great state for wild bird hunting, on one morning, a friend and I flushed 15 woodcock in the span of a few hours. I began to see how addicting hunting could be.

On January 2, 2021, I drove up to the WMA north of my house for a solo hunt. Zara and I walked through the woods and brushy areas where we'd seen woodcock over the past few weeks. After two hours, we'd only managed to bump one woodcock. I'd startled it as I walked into a thick area of woods. Zara was ahead of me and didn't even see it. Feeling annoyed, I decided it was time to leave. I recognized that this is one of the challenges of hunting—unlike with pen-raised birds, you have no idea where the birds are. Most of the time, that's the fun part. But it can also be frustrating.

I pulled out my camera to take a photo of Zara when my GPS tracker told me she was on point. After starting to hunt that season, I'd bought a tracking collar in order to keep tabs on Zara while we were hunting in thick cover. I put the camera down and hustled over to where the tracker indicated she was standing. She was on point in a briar patch near a clearing. I closed my shotgun and got ready to shoot. All of a sudden, the bird flushed into the clearing. I shot once, missed, and shot again. The bird went down in the clearing, and I was pretty sure I had hit it with my second shot. My heart was pounding.

"Zara, fetch!" I shouted. She ran over to where the bird went down and went on point again. Even though I was pretty sure I had hit it, I quickly reloaded my gun in case I needed to shoot again. When I reached her, I could tell that the bird was injured by the way it was flapping around. Zara sometimes pointed injured birds instead of picking them up right away. I encouraged her to fetch again, and she picked it up and brought it to me. I praised her effusively.

"Good girl, Zar! Look at you! What a good girl!" She paraded around me with the woodcock, clearly pleased with her prize. For once, I let her take a few victory laps. Eventually, I knelt down and took it from her. I held the small bird in my hand and savored the moment. I couldn't believe I'd actually managed to shoot one, and it was extra sweet since Zara had pointed and retrieved it. I carefully placed it in my vest and we headed back to the car.

I did not let my very first wild bird go to waste. When we got home, I carefully removed the breast and legs and cooked them for Chris and me to try. I took out the neck, heart, and liver, and froze them in a plastic bag for Zara to eat in a few weeks. I also saved multiple feathers. I mailed a few to a friend who loves birds and bird watching. The remaining feathers I had made into a pair of earrings. The artist was a fellow Vizsla owner with whom I connected through social media.

Hunting, it turned out, something I had been so resistant to in the past, was actually the culmination of my interest in watching Zara run freely. The first time I watched Zara run off-leash through the woods in 2014 had awakened something in me that found its ultimate expression in hunting. Here was an activity where Zara could run off-leash, legally, on public land, and all I had to do was follow along and watch her work. It was almost too good to be true.

I also felt a connection to my family history when I hunted. My paternal grandfather had been a hunter, and he was actually involved in running dogs in field trials. How I wished I could have met him, although by the time I started hunting, he had already been dead for 45 years.

Chapter 21

The Big Leagues

In the fall of 2020, with the Utility Test over, it was time to move on to something new. Like the previous year, I had my sights set on AKC Hunting Tests. This time, however, we were headed to the big leagues—Master Hunter. I knew that Zara could handle the requirements for steadiness and retrieving, but we would need help with backing. Even though I had tried to work on backing with her the previous season, somehow, another nine months had slipped by without us making much progress. I'd been too focused on trying to get her ready for the Utility Test.

I needed help teaching Zara to back other dogs. After Zara and I had received the Prize 2, I had talked to another chapter member, Stacy Horst, the night of the test. She mentioned that if I needed any help training in the future, I should reach out to her and her husband Blake. Both of them had just earned Prize 1 titles with their young GSPs and they trained dogs professionally. I decided to take her up on her offer.

In mid-December, we met up for the first time. Blake and Stacy lived about an hour south of me, and they trained at a farm that was owned by a friend of theirs. The farm housed their pigeon coop, quail/chukar house, and duck pen. There were two large fields for running dogs, a swamp for duck search, and a barn where we'd had NAVHDA events in the past. It was an ideal training location.

The first thing we did was make sure that Zara would stop-to-flush. Stacy also suggested that we do some stop-to-shot drills as well. This would ensure that she had the foundation in order to transition to backing other dogs. My work at Cripple Creek had paid off, and Zara stopped each time a pigeon was catapulted out of a launcher. As she was running ahead of us, Stacy also fired her blank pistol at random intervals to see if Zara would stop. Although I had not practiced stop-to-shot with Zara, she picked up on it quickly and began stopping as soon as the gun fired. She wagged her tail and looked around, probably searching for a fallen bird. Stop-to-shot is a beneficial exercise for bird dogs, because, if your dog is trained to stop when the gun goes off, they will be less likely to break on the gunshot and try to go after a bird. Breaking on the shot definitely was something I'd had issues with Zara in the past.

The next time I visited Blake and Stacy, they brought their older dog, Emma. They set up electronic launchers in the field loaded with pigeons. We ran Emma and Zara together in the field and got Emma to go on point first. Then, I encouraged Zara to come into the vicinity, and, if she didn't stop when she saw Emma, Blake would launch the bird. Since Zara knew how to stop-to-flush, this would make her stop without a command. They also recommended incorporating retrieving into the backing drills from the beginning. They thought that allowing the backing dog occasionally to retrieve often made them more willing to want to back. Retrieving was a reward.

On the first couple of times when Zara backed Emma due to the bird flushing from the launcher, Blake would throw a live quail in the air, shoot it, and tell me to send Zara to retrieve it. Emma stood during this exchange, waiting patiently for her turn. After Zara finished her retrieve, Emma would have a chance to retrieve as well.

After a few repetitions of this, Zara backed Emma without us flushing the bird first! I was thrilled. Soon, we started practicing with their other two dogs, a young male GSP named Porter and a young female named Arbor. Porter and Arbor were also training for Master Hunting Tests. One weekend, we went to a different property and practiced with a few other NAVHDA members. I noticed that Zara didn't back as quickly at this new location. I knew that dogs often don't transfer skills easily from place to place. Still, this worried me, because she would need to back other dogs at the hunting test grounds.

Thankfully, I had the opportunity to practice before Zara's first Master Hunting Test at the same location where the test was being held. It was at the Sandhills Pointing Breeds Club, where I had run Senior Hunter the year before. I drove there the Thursday before the test weekend. There were several other dog owners there with different breeds. Since the running order for the weekend had already been posted, I knew that Zara was running with a Weimaraner on Saturday and a German Wirehaired Pointer on Sunday. I was able to run her with both breeds as practice at SPBC. Unfortunately, she seemed hesitant to back the other dogs, almost like she was trying to avoid backing. If I was in the vicinity, she would eventually slow down and stop. But if she was far in front of me, she wouldn't slam to a stop if she was near the other dog. In retrospect, I think we went through the training process for backing too quickly. I had been in a rush because I had a test coming up. As a result, Zara did not have a solid enough foundation in the skill. Because of this, I would end up having to reteach and reinforce backing later on.

Going into our Master Hunting Test, I felt worried. I knew that she should be fine with the steadiness, retrieving, and the stop-to-flush, but I didn't know how the backing/honoring would go. Once she stopped, standing through the other dog's retrieve was usually not an issue. But I really hoped that she didn't bust in on another dog's point. That would be very embarrassing. I crossed my fingers that she would remember our training.

Zara was running in the sixth brace of the morning. When it was our turn, I gathered up all my gear and headed to the start line with Zara in tow. I carried my shotgun, unloaded and broken open on my shoulder. I also had my blank pistol in one of the front pockets of my hunting vest, to be used on birds in the back field that wouldn't be shot. I did feel somewhat nervous, but the presence of the shotgun gave me a boost of confidence. In Junior and Senior Hunting Tests, you do not carry a shotgun. In Master Hunting Tests, the handler has to swing at the bird when it flies and pretend they are shooting. Therefore, anyone looking at me would know that we were competing at the Master level. My clothes were a little more indicative of a bird hunter, too. When I ran Junior Hunter with Zara, I had worn black running tights and a running shirt, neither of which were great for walking through brush and briars. This time, I had on brush pants with reinforced fronts, an Orvis blaze orange hunting jacket, and knee-high boots, plus my bird hunting vest, a blaze orange hat, and earplugs. Of course, I also carried with me the weight of my expectations, which were much heavier to bear than they had been at the beginning. Five years into my hunting test journey with Zara, I was starting to feel like I belonged. I also looked more the part. We were not quite amateurs anymore.

I met my bracemate, a woman with a male Weimaraner. She told me that her dog already had several MH passes. We stood near the start line chatting until the judges signaled that it was time to release our dogs. Zara was amped and whining at the end of the leash. She knew what was about to happen.

Finally, it was time. Zara and the Weimaraner took off down the dirt road towards the fields. I hurried along to keep up. It was a cold day, and my fingers were numb inside my gloves. But cold weather is better for running dogs, so I didn't mind too much.

We reached the back field, and the judges told us to spend a few minutes letting our dogs search in this area. Suddenly, Zara went on point. I signaled to the judges and went in to flush the bird. I swapped my shotgun to my left shoulder and used my right hand to pull my blank pistol out of my pocket. When I purchased my own blank pistol a few years ago, I had purposefully chosen one with an easy trigger. I had no trouble firing this one. Thankfully, I quickly found the bird and kicked it up. Zara watched patiently as it flew away. I fired a blank shot, and she didn't move a muscle. *Good girl*, I thought.

"March!" I commanded and I heeled her away from the bird. After we got a good distance away, I released her. She took off running towards the bird field, so I also headed that way. *So far, so good.*

I followed her into the bird field and stayed to the left of the dirt road. The Weim and his handler walked on the right side of the road. Zara went on point again. This time, since we were in the bird field, one of the gunners walked up to us after I called the point. He got in position, and I walked in to flush the bird. It got up, but the gunner missed, and the bird landed near the woodline in front of us. Zara held still but was staring intently at where the bird had gone down. I walked back to her and sternly commanded her to heel away. Soon she was back hunting again.

After a nonproductive point, Zara ran back toward the woods where the previous quail had landed. She went on point, and I assumed it was the bird we had seen before. Again, the gunner approached us and got ready to shoot. I knew it was going to be a difficult shot because the bird was right on the edge of the woods. Not surprisingly, the gunner missed as the quail flew into the woods. I sighed, and heeled Zara away. Thankfully, she was listening really well to me.

We continued walking through the field, and Zara found a fourth bird. When I flushed the bird, it flew towards the judges, so the gunner didn't shoot for safety reasons. At this point, I had lost track of time, but we had been out there for a while. She still needed to honor the other dog and get a retrieve. The Weimaraner went on point, and the judges signaled for me to bring Zara into the vicinity. I took a deep breath and called her over. She ran toward me, glanced to her right where the Weim was standing and *stopped*. I cheered silently. I approached her and whispered, "Good girl! Whoa."

I stood next to Zara as the Weimaraner's handler flushed the bird. It flew into the air, and the gunners shot it. I noticed, however, that the Weim did not see where it landed. He was looking in the other direction. The handler released him, and he bounded forward, searching intently. Zara stayed next to me, watching closely. The Weim continued to search in vain. The handler tried to help him by lining him up in the right direction and sending him to fetch again. At this point, Zara had been honoring him for several minutes. She kept glancing back at me as if to say, "Seriously? I have to stand and watch this?"

There's a line in the AKC rulebook for pointing breed hunting tests that states if the pointing dog takes an excessively long time to retrieve, the judges can let the backing dog move on. As Zara started to look at me, I kept checking the judges to see if they would let me release her, but I didn't want to say anything, because I feared if I spoke, she would break. Finally, after what felt like an eternity, the Weim managed to find the quail and bring it back. "Free!" I said to Zara, and she took off. I couldn't believe she'd managed to honor for that long.

After finding two more birds that spontaneously flushed so they couldn't be shot, she went on point for a seventh time. This time, the Weim needed to honor Zara. The owner called him over; he saw Zara and headed in the other direction. *This is going to be a while*, I thought with annoyance. Zara was steady on point and not creeping. She looked at me like, "Aren't you going to flush this bird?"

"Good girl, whoa," I whispered. The Weim circled around her a few more times, with the owner trying desperately to get him to stop. Finally, one of the judges told her to hold his collar.

"He's already blinked the back several times," the judge said with annoyance. "Just collar him so we can get this retrieve done." The Weimaraner's handler grumbled but did what he said.

Zara had been on point for several minutes. I couldn't believe how patient she was being. Both gunners approached, and I stepped in to flush the bird. I was grateful that they did not miss the shot. Zara perked up when it fell, but didn't move.

"Fetch!" I said, and she bounded toward the quail. She picked it up and started looking like she wanted to head in the other direction with her prize. "Zara, come," I said firmly, and she returned right to me. I took the quail and praised her. We had made it through our first Master Hunting Test with flying colors.

The judges and the gunners circled around me as I leashed up Zara. "She did such a great job!" one of them said.

"I know," I said breathlessly. "That was amazing."

"Did you train her yourself?" one of the judges asked.

"Yes, I did," I said. "With some help from other NAVHDA members."

"Congratulations!"

I thanked them and walked Zara back down to the parking area. She had blown me away with her obedience that day. I had flashbacks to her very first Junior Hunting Test, when I had shown up without any expectations and was rewarded with an A+ performance. This time, I hadn't been certain she was ready for the Master level, but she had shown me that, without a doubt, she could hang with the big dogs.

She received high scores for that performance. Her score for honoring, that part I'd been most worried about, was a 10 out of 10. She also got a 10 in hunting, and 9s in every other category. I was happy.

On Sunday, we returned for the second day of the two-day test. After crushing it on Saturday, I had a feeling that she was not going to do as well. Sure enough, on her second bird contact, I could not find the bird.

Looking for the bird is one of the more stressful parts of hunting tests for me, especially if it takes a long time. Everyone is watching you and waiting anxiously for the bird to appear. In the past, I've been able to relocate Zara without any problem. Sometimes when a bird dog establishes a point, they may be quite far from the bird, which can make it difficult for the handler to find. A dog can be taught to relocate by giving them a command, and that gives them the opportunity to get closer to the scent/bird and point again, which may make it easier to find the bird.

So, after kicking around in the grass for several minutes, I gave her a "free" command, which told her to break point and reestablish herself closer to the bird. She moved past me, and, suddenly, a quail flushed into the sky. Her original point had been a fair distance from the bird.

As the bird flushed, Zara took several steps towards it. Out of habit, I said "Whoa!" She stopped, but I knew that wasn't allowed in Master Hunting Tests. I turned around and looked at the judges with a knowing look on my face.

"I'm sorry," one of them said.

"It's okay," I replied. "At least I know what we have to work on." This was the exact same problem I'd encountered with Zara at the Utility Test the previous fall—if she encountered a bird and I wasn't close by, she wanted to chase it instead of stopping. *Time to do more stop-to-flush and electronic-launcher work*, I thought. But at least we had gotten one Master Hunter pass that weekend. We only needed four more. Dogs without a Senior Hunter title need six passes to get a Master Hunter title. Since Zara already had the SH title, she only needed five passes total.

Chapter 22

BHAG

Shortly after our first weekend of Master Hunting Tests, the Vizsla Club of America released the premium for their 2021 National Gun Dog Championship (NGDC). Entries were due on March 8th. I reached out to Melissa Thomas, who was serving as the test secretary for the event, and asked if there was a limit on the number of entries they would accept. "No," she said. "It's not a limited entry. We take entries up until the deadline." *Oh good*, I thought. I told her that I was planning to enter if we could get Zara's Master Hunter title in time. But I wouldn't know that until the weekend of February 27–28th.

I looked at my calendar and planned out the tests we would have to enter in order to meet the deadline. There was a double hunting test in Chester, South Carolina the weekend of February 13–14th. The Sandhills Pointing Breed Club was having another one the last weekend in February. However, I saw that the Conestoga Vizsla Club was having a double-double hunting test in Delaware that same weekend. That meant four chances in two days. It was a six-hour drive from Raleigh. Despite the distance, I knew I needed to travel to that event. Even though Zara needed just four more passes, I had to assume that we would fail at least once or twice. And, as a last resort, there was one more double hunting test in Chester the first weekend of March. I sent my entries into all these tests in January, knowing that they filled up fast. I could always cancel the last one if we didn't need it.

We would be cutting it close, but I still had hope that we could qualify in time to attend the NGDC. When I was thinking of entering in 2020, I had felt an intense sense of imposter syndrome. *The NGDC is not for people like me*, I thought. It was for seasoned field trial competitors who knew the game and had the titles to prove it. Zara had never even been to a field trial, and I was certainly not qualified either. I was still so new to the bird dog world; I had no idea what I was doing half the time. I didn't want people to look at us and think we were silly for entering such a big event.

But after having another year to mull it over, as well as to refine Zara's training, I had started to feel a little better about entering. I was not really a newbie anymore. I had trained Zara and earned a Prize 2 in the rigorous Utility Test. I might as well aim high, right? I realized that I often perform better with ambitious goals. Those are the ones that keep me motivated, versus goals that are easier to achieve. There's an acronym used in the business world when companies set ambitious goals for themselves: BHAG. It stands for Big, Hairy, Audacious Goal.

I decided not to let my BHAG to get Zara to the NGDC intimidate me. After all, it was no different than some of the other things I'd set out to do. Taking an untrained four-year-old Vizsla and teaching her steadiness, how to retrieve, and the concept of duck search in preparation for the Utility Test certainly qualified as a BHAG as well.

In order to feel more prepared, I spent a fair amount of time scouring the archives of the NGDC on the Vizsla Club of America's website. They posted results from the past 10 years. Some years had detailed scribe notes that explained what went on in each brace. I found these write-ups especially interesting. I would look at the dogs who placed and see what went on during their brace. What made them so special? There wasn't a clear answer, but I still found it enlightening to read them. I also saw that a lot of the dogs didn't make it through the full hour.

During the latter part of January, I trained a little more with Blake and Stacy before Zara's next hunting test. I had noticed that Zara was sometimes a bit slow to honor the other dog if I was not in the vicinity. Ideally, she should back the other dog as soon as she saw it, regardless of whether or not I was there. If I called her around, and she knew I was watching, she would stop. This worried me a bit going into our next test, but I hoped for the best.

Early on the morning of February 13th, I loaded Zara up in my car and drove about three hours to Chester, South Carolina. The temperature hovered right around freezing, and it was raining. As I drove in the weak morning light, I worried that the roads would start to ice over and become slick. The forecast was calling for rain all weekend. Eventually, we made it there safely.

When we arrived, it was 35 degrees and raining. I spoke to the test secretary and learned that many of the Master-level dogs weren't passing because the birds were not flying. Instead of waiting for the handler to flush, dogs were diving in and taking out the birds themselves. Prior to the test, a friend had warned me that wet birds often smell like dead birds. *Yikes*, I thought. However, Zara and I had trained in the rain before, and I had never seen her try to pick up a wet bird.

We waited around for a little while until it was Zara's turn to run. The weather was pretty miserable. Zara was not a fan of cold rain, and she shivered while we waited. The two judges rode up on horses and asked if we were ready to go. They told the other handler and me that we were going to go straight to the bird field instead of spending a lot of time in the back field since the weather was so terrible. I released Zara, and she ran down the hill, but she was moving slower than normal due to the rain. I started walking toward the bird field, and she headed there too, quickly locking up on a bird.

I signaled to the judges that she was on point, and the gunners got in position. I tried to flush the bird, but it was wet and wouldn't fly. One of the gunners shot it on the ground. *That works,* I thought, and sent Zara to retrieve.

After the retrieve was complete, I tried to hustle her out of the bird field so that the other handler would have a chance to get his dog on a bird. On the way out, she went on point again. *Of course this happens*, I thought. One of the gunners left our bracemate and came over to where Zara was standing. I tried to flush the bird, but like the previous one, it wouldn't fly and started walking. The gunner told me to blank it using my pistol. Since Zara had already retrieved, the judges didn't need to see another one. "Okay," I said, and fired the blank. Zara was staring the bird down. "March," I commanded firmly and walked her in the opposite direction.

The rain continued to fall. I was wearing gloves, but they had soaked through, and my hands were freezing as I held my shotgun on my shoulder. All I needed was for Zara to back the other dog. We bided our time away from the birds until the judges called that the other dog was on point. It was a male Weimaraner, and Zara had a good view of him as we approached. The other handler stood back as I tried to bring Zara around. She slowed down and looked around as if she could escape this situation. *Come on, Zara,* I thought. Finally, she stopped moving, and I quickly went over to her. Unlike at our test in January, this dog's retrieve was efficient, and Zara did not have to honor for a long time. After that, the judges thanked us, and the other handler and I slowly made our way up the hill to the start of the course. I was pleased that Zara had done well despite the bad weather conditions.

That afternoon, I checked into our hotel. Zara still looked very energetic, so I decided to take her to a nearby wildlife management area where she could run around and burn some energy. It was still cold and raining, but I didn't want to have to deal with an underexercised Vizsla in the hotel that night. I also hoped that it would help her be less crazy in the morning for the next test. Unfortunately, that was not the case. Like the previous year, when we had done a two-day test at this same location, she was fired up on Sunday morning. At least the weather was a little better.

When it was finally time to release her, she shot down the hill in mere seconds. I hustled to keep up. Soon after, she went on point next to a tree that was right outside the bird field. Before I could get close enough to flush, the bird flew a few feet off the ground and then started walking in front of Zara. She didn't budge. *Oh good girl,* I thought. This was the scenario that had done us in during our second Master Hunting Test, as well as at the Utility Test.

I chased after the bird to get it to fly, and after a few seconds, it took off. I returned to Zara and heeled her away. A few minutes later, she went on a point on another bird that was walking. She was staunch. Since we were still not in the bird field, I blanked it and heeled her away. The word "*easy*" popped into my mind. This was what we had been training for all this time: situations where I had complete control and she was behaving like a finished dog. It turned out that the key was consistency. Regular training sessions on live birds had finally made Zara dependably steady.

We made it into the bird field, and Zara went on point for a third time. This time, the gunners came up beside me, and I was able to flush it. Unlike the day before, it was not raining, so the birds were flying a little better. The gunners hit the bird, and I sent Zara for the retrieve. She brought it back, and I praised her. We were halfway done with the test. "Okay, now just keep her out of trouble," one of the judges joked.

Her bracemate was a slow-moving Gordon Setter. The Gordon went on point near a clump of high grass. I called Zara into the vicinity, and she stopped beside me. Unfortunately, when the bird flushed, the gunners could not shoot because it would have been an unsafe situation. I sighed, dreading the fact that Zara would have to back again. I released her and she quickly found a fourth bird. The bird field was full of birds from the previous day's test. I looked at the judges and gunners to see if they were going to come shoot it, but they told me to blank it instead. Annoyed, I shot my blank pistol and heeled Zara away.

"Point!" the Gordon's handler called. I looked up and saw that the Gordon was standing still.

"Zara, this way!" I said. She headed towards me and stopped when she saw the other dog. "Good girl," I said. The other handler went in to flush but couldn't find the bird. *You have got to be kidding me*, I thought. *Zara is going to have to back for a third time?!*

It had begun to rain lightly. I released Zara, and she went back to hunting, because, after all, this was a hunting test. She found a fifth and a sixth bird, both of which I blanked. I heeled her off, but I could tell that she really wanted a retrieve. She was looking frustrated that the birds weren't being shot.

"I told you to keep her out of trouble!" The judge said to me, half-joking. I looked at him with an expression of helplessness on my face. *How am I supposed to contain this dog? I trained her to find birds and that is what she's doing!* I thought.

The judge told me to stand still until the other dog went on point. *Fine*, I thought with annoyance. I put Zara in a whoa next to me. Finally, the Gordon Setter went on point for a third time. Zara was slow to back the other dog, which was not surprising given the situation.

The handler flushed the bird, and the gunners shot. As the bird went down, Zara took a hop forward. She wanted that bird. "Whoa!" I cried. She stopped. I looked back at the judges, my heart sinking. We had made it so far in this crazy test, could we really fail at the last second?

But, thankfully, she passed. She earned a low score in honoring, but that was to be expected. The fact that she handled so much pressure was hard to believe. Not only did she have to honor three separate times, but also she found multiple birds and only got the satisfaction of one retrieve.

After the test was over, we left quickly, ready to escape the bad weather. We had three passes down and only needed two more.

Chapter 23

Just in Time

By the end of February, we were only about a month away from the National Gun Dog Championship. I felt antsy not knowing if we would be able to go or not. Finally, the last weekend in February arrived, and Zara and I drove to Felton, Delaware for the Conestoga Vizsla Club's double-double hunting test. It was another cold, rainy weekend. But I wasn't too worried, knowing how Zara had done at the Chester hunting test.

We arrived early and were immediately welcomed by one of the hunting test volunteers. It was nice being at a test with many other Vizslas. Over the past few years, I had become used to Zara being the sole Vizsla. Most of the dogs in NAVHDA were German Shorthaired Pointers, German Wirehaired Pointers, or Wirehaired Pointing Griffons. Zara was paired with a Spinone, another less common breed, for our first brace. We set off, boots squishing in the soft, muddy ground. The judges were on horseback behind us.

We walked for what seemed like *forever* to get to the bird field. *Where are we going?!* I kept thinking. I had not been to a hunting test that had such a long back course. After several opportunities, it was clear that Zara didn't want to honor, so we got picked up toward the end of the first brace. I felt a little annoyed, because I wasn't positive that she had seen the other dog go on point. Zara generally ignored her bracemate when hunting and was focused on finding birds, not watching the other dog. Even though we only needed two more passes going into the weekend, I was glad I had entered all four tests.

There was a lunch break between the morning and afternoon tests, and I walked over to the lodge where they were serving food. I had been in touch with my uncle Richard, who lived about an hour from the test site in southern Delaware. He had told me he was interested in coming to the hunting test. As I was walking across the parking lot, I saw him pull up in a blue pickup truck.

I had not seen him in several years, and I was happy that he came. This was the first time I had seen him since I started hunting and had gotten deep into the bird dog world with Zara. For a long time, he had been the only person I knew who actually hunted, and I was excited to discuss hunting and bird dogs with him. When I was in elementary school, he had had two Brittanies named Duke and Duchess. He told me that he had run one of them in a few field trials, which was something I didn't know. We discussed hunting and how he had trained his dogs. He seemed impressed that I had trained Zara myself and jumped into hunting tests without a lot of prior knowledge.

After lunch, I said goodbye to Uncle Richard and got ready for Zara's second run of the day. As expected, she was energized and ready to go. This time, the GSP she was running with went on point in the back course, and, since the judges seemed to want to see the dogs honor each other at every opportunity, I made sure to call her around and get her in a good position to honor on her own. She saw the GSP and stopped, which made me breathe a sigh of relief.

Thankfully, the judges shortened the course for the afternoon, so we didn't have to hike as far. Zara was running big, and I was practically jogging to keep up with her. The remainder of the test went smoothly, though, and she easily passed.

Sunday was another cold and wet day. The birds weren't flying well, which seemed to be the theme of our Master Hunting Test journey. I noticed that Zara was getting a little loose on the birds, needing more correction than she had during the first test Saturday morning. This was probably because I had run her three times on Saturday. After our first two runs, they had an uneven number of dogs and needed an extra "bye dog" to run with a male Vizsla. I figured it wouldn't hurt and volunteered.

Despite that, she passed the test on Sunday morning, and, with that fifth pass, earned her Master Hunter title. I was thrilled. A little more than five years after she'd first done so well at the Conestoga Vizsla Club's Junior Hunting Test in Sumerduck, Virginia, we completed her

Master Hunter title, fittingly enough, at another Conestoga Test. It had been a long journey, but we were headed to the National Gun Dog Championship! I couldn't wait to get home so I could email my entry form to Melissa that night.

Chapter 24

Making a Plan

N ow that Zara had her Master Hunter title, it was time to focus on getting ready for the NGDC. We had three weeks until the event kicked off on Monday, March 22nd. I had never been to the place where the NGDC would be held, but the Old Dominion Vizsla Club was holding a field trial at the same location the first weekend of March. I knew I needed to attend. It would be invaluable to be able to run Zara on the same course as the one she would need to complete in the NGDC. Plus, Zara had never been in a finished Gun Dog Stake at a field trial before.

That weekend, I drove the 3 hours and 20 minutes to Caret, Virginia. Zara was scheduled to run in the Amateur Gun Dog Stake on Sunday. Although it was primarily an event where handlers rode horses, they allowed walking handlers as well. I had actually taken horseback riding lessons when I was in middle school, but given that 20 years had passed, I did not feel comfortable riding a horse, let alone trying to handle Zara off of one. I figured walking would be fine.

Early on Sunday morning, I drove to the field trial after spending the night at a nearby hotel. The trial was located at Blandfield Plantation, a beautiful and massive private property along the Rappahannock River in eastern Virginia. Zara's breeder, Jane, was there with Zara's littermate Benny. There were four more of Zara's relatives there as well. Melissa, who had originally encouraged me to enter the NGDC, had Zara's half-brother Boss, who was almost 10, and Connor, who was three. Additionally, a couple named Shawn and Maria were there with two more half-brothers, Fen, who was six, and Lou, who was almost one. All of these dogs shared Bull as a sire. It would be the same story at the NGDC, with several Bull offspring in attendance. Zara enjoyed flirting with her siblings while we waited for her turn to run.

I was able to watch Benny and Melissa's younger dog, Conner, run the course. Both Jane and Melissa were running their dogs off horseback. Watching those braces, I was amazed at how far the dogs ran away from their handlers. *Yikes, Zara and I really have some work to do*, I thought. Before coming to this trial, I thought she liked to range far, but apparently my sense of distance was relative.

After finishing Zara's Master Hunter title a week ago, we had not done much training. At the ODVC field trial, Zara ran in the sixth brace with an Irish Red and White Setter. The Setter's handler was also walking, which was a relief. I would have felt much more anxious if I had needed to keep up with a horseback handler.

The course began in the woods and led out into open fields. Zara started slowly, hardly ranging from me. It almost seemed like she didn't know she was supposed to be hunting, which was unusual. However, she got around clean, which means that she didn't make any mistakes that would have disqualified her during the 30-minute run. She found one quail and handled it well. Toward the end of the course, she was hunting in the cornfields when suddenly, a large male pheasant flushed in front of her. She slowed to a stop as I stared in wonder. Then, four more pheasants flew up farther away from her. It was a beautiful sight to see such large birds in person. I shot my blank pistol and walked quickly towards her. Zara had never seen a pheasant while hunting before, let alone five, and she had performed like an old pro by executing a flawless stop-to-flush. It was incredible.

At the end of the 30 minutes, the judge congratulated me on getting around clean, especially considering it was our first time. "Have I seen you before?" he asked, looking at me quizzically.

"Yes," I replied, realizing who he was. "You judged Zara in her first Junior Hunter test five years ago. Her sire is Laura Miller's Bull."

"Ah," he said. "You've got a special pup, then."

"Yes, I know," I said, smiling at Zara.

I was not surprised that Zara didn't place at the field trial. She had not ranged well, and I knew that was important in the field trial world.

However, attending the event had been invaluable. As I drove home that afternoon, I made a mental list of all the things I needed to work on prior to the National Gun Dog Championship, which was now only two weeks away.

- I needed to train Zara to stay out in front of me.

- I needed to train her to the whistle, which would help me keep her out in front and be able to turn her from a distance.

- I needed to condition her to the warmer weather. It had been sunny and 49 degrees at the field trial. While that is not hot, I realized that for almost all of the hunt tests we had run, it had been mid-30s and raining. Even 49 and sunny was a big difference compared to that.

- I also needed to work on my power-walking skills. Even though I was in good shape from running, walking rapidly to keep up with a fast-moving Vizsla across uneven terrain was not an easy task. I knew that walking quickly would also help push her out.

Of course, I recognized that I only had so much time. I could not work miracles in two weeks. But I was going to try.

Chapter 25

Factors I Could Control

On Monday afternoon, after returning from the field trial, I took Zara and Colombo to the public dove fields about a half-hour from my house. It was a large piece of property that would allow me to work on Zara's range. I pulled my whistle out of the dog training gear box I kept in my car. I had bought the whistle before Zara's first Junior Hunting Test. I had briefly used it for recall with her when she was younger. But I had stopped using it after joining NAVHDA, because she was never that far from me, and she listened well enough without it. Having the e-collar helped with her listening skills as well. But now it was time to reacquaint her with the tool.

I walked past the gate to the dove fields with both dogs on leash. After we got 10 yards into the property, I released Colombo and held Zara's collar. "Zara, find the birds," I said. "Go!" I commanded and blew the whistle once. I let go of her collar and she took off in front of me. Colombo trotted along beside me. He was just along for the ride.

I had started using the phrase "find the birds" when we went woodcock hunting. Woodcock are usually found in the woods, not in open fields like pen-raised quail and chukar. I found that hunting in wooded areas was not something that came naturally to her, so I started using that term to switch her from just running around to actually hunting.

After talking to Jane, I had decided to implement two whistle commands—one blast to keep her in front of me ("go"), and two blasts to turn her ("this way"). She was familiar with "go" and "this way," so I used the verbal commands first, followed by the whistle, to build the association.

Zara was running ahead of me down the dirt path. After she got about 75 yards in front, she turned around and started heading back to me, which was her natural tendency. As soon as she turned towards me, I called out, "Go!" and blew on the whistle. I also used my arm to motion her to move forward. She slowed down and then headed away from me. "Good girl!" I cried.

We walked through fields that had grown corn the previous year. The rows of dead cornstalks provided a good edge. Dogs in field trials are encouraged to run along the edges of fields or woods, since that is typically where the birds are. So that's what I wanted to train Zara to do. No more wandering around open fields in circles like we had done in the hunting tests.

I also tried to keep her in front of me, between "10 and 2," if you think about the face of a clock. I used the command "this way" and the two whistle blasts to do this.

We continued this training for about 30 minutes. Given that it was close to 70 degrees, I didn't want to overexert her on one of the first warm days of spring. But I was happy with how she had done. It seemed like she was starting to pick up on the commands and get what I wanted her to do. I had also been walking quickly the whole time to work on my own training.

I ran Zara on leash several times over the next two weeks. This would also help with her heat endurance, I hoped. I was lucky that we lived south of the trial site, in an area that was experiencing warmer weather before the event. Given that it was a national event with people coming from all over the country, I knew that not everyone would have this luxury.

As I thought more about the NGDC, I realized that I needed to focus on the things I could control. I knew I couldn't control the other dogs. While I wasn't sure if she had the range to be on the same level with these field trial Vizslas, she would not be picked up for staying close to me or running slowly. However, if Zara made a mistake on a bird, such as taking steps on the flush, or breaking on the shot, she would be done. Therefore, I needed to make sure her bird work was flawless. I could control that by having as many productive training sessions on birds as possible before the event. Thanks to my NAVHDA connections, I was able to train three times over the two weeks with live quail. I met up with

Stacy twice before the event, at a larger property where she had access. She planted the quail along the edges of the woods, as I requested, and I tried to run Zara in a straight line using my whistle. I shot my blank pistol for most of the birds, and Stacy shot one with her shotgun, which imitated how the NGDC would be run.

In an interesting turn of events, I also met up with Ozzie Osborne at the Sandhills Pointing Breeds Club. After turning down Ozzie's offer to train Zara in 2017, I had reconnected with him at a NAVHDA duck search clinic in 2020. He was venturing into the NAVHDA world with his GSP, Thor, who was already a Master Hunter. I had gone woodcock hunting with him once in January. I had mentioned to him that I was trying to qualify Zara for the NGDC, and, if so, I might need his help. Even though field trials were not his forte, he was willing to have me as a guest at SPBC.

He invited me to come to SPBC on the Friday morning before we headed to the NGDC. Ozzie showed me a route that I could run Zara, which would simulate a field trial course. He helped me plant several quail, and I got Zara ready to run. After releasing Zara, I walked behind her while Ozzie trailed us in an ATV. I tried to keep her in front of me and moving forward, which she did well for the most part. She found all three quail, and even though they weren't flying very well, she held her stance and didn't move until I walked back to her and grabbed her collar.

On Monday, March 22nd, I drove to Caret, Virginia. Chris was planning to come up to watch Zara run the next day and then head to DC for work. We arrived at Blandfield Plantation at midday and drove onto the grounds. Pickup trucks, campers, and horse trailers lined the dirt road leading into the property, and the Vizsla Club of America had set up headquarters for the event in two large, open tents. The COVID-19 pandemic was still going on, and many of the participants, including myself, had not yet been vaccinated. The VCA was trying to be as safe as possible by not holding any activities inside and keeping everyone spaced out.

The Puppy Classic had happened that morning. Puppies up to 15 months were eligible to run in the 20-minute stake, which was judged by field trial rules. The puppies didn't necessarily have to find birds. The judges were looking at their running style and hunting ability. As

I arrived, they were announcing the placements and photographing the dogs and their owners on an arrangement of hay bales.

I checked in with the event chair and then went to see Jane. She had been there since the weekend, helping to set up. That afternoon, I watched the Running of the Veterans. This was a just-for-fun event for dogs eight and older who were no longer in active competition. All of the dogs ran together and found birds, although they weren't being judged for anything. Zara's mother, Caiya, who was now 11 and white in the face, participated. I walked along behind the owners to watch the dogs. It was fun to see the older dogs run and display their bird manners. It was pretty hot, and, by the end, most of them had slowed down quite a bit.

After that was over, I asked Jane if she would help me train Zara on birds one last time. The VCA had allowed participants to pre-order quail to be used for training at the event. They had a small training field near the parking area where you could run your dog off-leash and plant birds. The field was long and narrow and started at the top of a hill. I had ordered four quail. I planted them in a line along the edge of the field as Jane held Zara at the top of the hill. After I finished, I returned to them and took Zara by the collar. I blew my whistle and released her. She took off, quickly finding the quail. Although she was steady, she was trying to take steps after I flushed them, which was not ideal. Jane encouraged me to use a verbal "whoa" if needed. I was used to not giving commands after running the NAVHDA Utility Test and AKC Master Hunting Tests, but she reminded me that saying "whoa" is okay in AKC field trials. "All right," I said with a sigh. I was hoping that a less than stellar "dress rehearsal" meant that Zara's performance would be better the next day.

Around 5pm, I left the grounds to check into my hotel, which was about 15 minutes away. I was thankful that I had taken the whole week off of work, so I didn't have to worry about responding to emails and finishing up projects. I could focus on relaxing and getting a good night's sleep before Zara ran in the morning.

Chapter 26

The National Gun Dog Championship

Tuesday morning dawned sunny and clear, with the promise of warm weather in the afternoon. I headed to Blandfield Plantation around 7:30am. Zara was running in the fourth brace, and I wanted to be able to watch at least one set of dogs before it was our turn. Jane was running Zara's brother Benny in the third brace.

The VCA had a horse wrangler for the trial, and people could rent horses to ride to watch the dogs run. However, for those of us who were not comfortable riding horses, they had a gallery wagon. This contraption consisted of a heavy-duty pickup truck with an aluminum structure in the place of its bed. There were steps up to two long bench seats on top, which sat about eight people. During each brace of the competition, someone would drive the gallery wagon through the field, following the course, so that spectators could ride along and watch. Dog boxes underneath the benches provided a place for a handler to put their dog if they got picked up in the middle of their run. I was thankful to have the gallery wagon as an option. Although the route it took was not always right next to the dogs, it did afford a pretty good view of the whole course.

I hopped on the gallery wagon to watch the first brace. I wanted to familiarize myself with the course at least once more before it was Zara's turn to compete. The first two dogs took off around 8am. One of them got picked up pretty quickly, due to some infraction on a bird that those of us in the gallery wagon couldn't see. The remaining dog, an older female, carried on and finished the whole hour. She found seven birds, which gave me pause. *That's a lot of birds*, I thought. *I hope Zara can handle herself.* Since most of the birds weren't being shot, I knew that by the time Zara ran, there would be even more birds out in the field. Then, again, Zara had found that many birds in the span of a half-hour hunting test and been fine.

After the first brace, I got off the gallery wagon and went to exercise Zara and Colombo in the training field before Jane's brace started. I thought I had plenty of time, but both dogs got picked up in that brace, which moved up the start time of the third brace significantly. Because of that, I wasn't able to watch Benny run. He did make it around clean, though, and Jane seemed pleased with his performance when she came back.

The judges took a lunch break and announced that the fourth brace would commence around 1pm. By this point, Chris had arrived. I was happy that he had come to watch Zara's performance. Although I had fallen hard into the world of dog sports, I knew that he did not enjoy being at these types of events as much as I did, so I appreciated him being there. He understood that it was a special occasion for Zara and me.

I tried to eat my lunch but had trouble eating much due to nerves. Although I had run in multiple hunting tests prior to the NGDC, I still got nervous beforehand. I just wanted to get on the course and begin, because I knew that my nerves would settle down once we started.

Finally, it was time to load up Zara in the gallery wagon and head to the start of the course. Zara's bracemate was a four-year-old female vizsla. Her owner told me that she had recently placed at a field trial in Florida, which allowed her to qualify for the NGDC. I was thankful that my bracemate was not one of the more seasoned competitors, because I would have felt even more intimidated being paired with a dog who already had national titles.

After one of the event volunteers announced our names, it was time to release the dogs. The judges rode behind us on horses, along with a horseback gallery of about 10 people. The gallery wagon was loaded with spectators, including Chris. I blew my whistle, let Zara go, and she took off, running hard, along the edge of the field. Her bracemate ran forward along the right edge of the same strip. As we walked, Zara started bearing to the left. I remembered the advice I'd gotten from the owner of Zara's sire to keep her between "10 and 2" if possible. I blew two short blasts on my whistle ("this way!") to get her back on course.

160

She was ranging pretty well, and we were off to a good start. I was walking briskly, but trying not to outpace the other handler. We were supposed to stay together if possible. About 10 minutes in, Zara's bracemate went on point at an area the VCA had deemed "Spectre's Berm." She was ahead of Zara to my right in the direction we were headed. *Oh no,* I thought with a sinking feeling. *I'm going to have to get her to honor.* Since Zara had been somewhat hesitant to honor during her last hunting tests, I wasn't thrilled about her having to do it, especially so early into the run. But I didn't want it to look like I was avoiding the honor, so I figured I better call Zara into the vicinity and just get it over with. I could whoa her if needed. In field trials, unlike Master Hunting Tests, your dog doesn't have to honor to earn a placement. You can also command them into a back, similar to Senior Hunter.

Just as I was about to give Zara a "this way" command, the other handler passed close by me on the way to her dog. "You should go on," she said to me firmly in a voice that the judges couldn't hear. The way she was looking out for me caught me off-guard, but I decided to heed her advice. Thankfully, Zara soon went on point in the same area but far enough away from her bracemate that it was obviously a different bird.

I walked up next to Zara and gave her a quiet "whoa." I knew that the gunners would try to shoot this bird, so I waited for them to arrive. At first, I thought that they would shoot her bracemate's bird first, and Zara would have to stand through that, but I quickly saw that there were two sets of gunners. Once the two men reached us, I confirmed that they were ready, and I moved in to flush the bird. It flew a short distance and one of the gunners shot it as it was drifting back to the ground. I paused and gave Zara a fetch command. She bounded toward the bird with enthusiasm and took a second or two to pick it up. I was tempted to call "come" but I resisted the urge. *Don't give extra commands if you don't have to.* Zara returned to me with the bird in her mouth, and I took it from her without any issues. As I turned around to give it to the gunners, I saw that both judges were standing close behind me on horseback.

"It's just you now," one of them said.

"Oh, okay," I replied with surprise. I glanced over to where her bracemate and the other handler had been. Apparently she had gotten picked up. I was relieved that I wouldn't have to worry about Zara honoring anymore. I gave Zara some water and could tell that she was already getting hot. It was probably about 60 degrees, and the sun was shining. I held her collar, walked her a short distance away from where the bird had been, and let her go.

I walked fast around the edges of the course, knowing that the faster I walked, the more it would push Zara out. She found another quail about five minutes later. I walked in, flushed it, and fired my blank pistol. I watched Zara's face carefully as the bird flew away, ready to give a corrective command if she tried to budge. I had been worried that she may be tempted to break on subsequent birds after being able to retrieve the first one. She held still, and I gave a firm "whoa" as I returned to her and grabbed her collar. In field trials, dogs are held by the collar and physically moved away from a bird, unlike Master Hunter tests, where you have to heel the dog off-leash away from an unshot bird. I had spent a lot of time releasing Zara by touching her body and I didn't want her to bolt as I touched her collar. As the trial went on, this turned into me almost pouncing on her as I got close. She never tried to break, but I wasn't taking any chances—probably not the best look, but it worked.

We continued on, and she was getting hot. I felt like I was constantly giving her water. I would blow my whistle to keep her out in front of me, but every few minutes I would call her back to have a drink. Since Jane was scouting for me, she was able to carry some extra water bottles on her horse. This was helpful, since it would have been difficult for me to carry enough water for the full hour. In field trials, you are allowed to designate one other person on horseback as a "scout." The job of this person is to help locate your dog when it's on point and help find your dog if you lose track of them.

We entered the field that was known to hold pheasants. Although she had successfully stopped-to-flush on what was essentially a covey of pheasants at the field trial two weeks prior, I wanted to avoid pheasants if at all possible. I tried to keep her out of the left side of that field, which was where the pheasants had been in the past. She started getting birdy, which I was able to discern by her fast-moving tail and quick back-and-forth motion. However, she also started to bounce a few times, which was a behavior I'd seen when she encountered other animals that were not birds, such as rabbits and mice. *That's not what we're looking for, Zara,*

I thought. She stopped moving, and I called the point, although I soon wished I hadn't. She didn't look as staunch as she should have been, which meant that there probably wasn't a bird there. But I had to try to find it. I kicked all around the whole area but, unsurprisingly, could not find a bird. Instead of asking the judges if I could relocate her, I walked back to her and said, "free," which is her release word. She broke the point and started sniffing around. Feeling sure that there wasn't a bird, I encouraged her to keep moving.

I immediately regretted how I'd handled that whole sequence. I hoped that the judges didn't think that she'd broken point on her own. They may not have been able to hear the release command I'd given her. I groaned internally. Oh well, I had to keep going. We still had more than 30 minutes left. I was sweating, and Zara was very hot. I could tell she was starting to slow down. She found a small puddle and looked like she wanted to bathe in it. Instead, she peed in it. The judges then pointed out that there was a pond just up ahead.

"Oh, great," I said, and encouraged Zara to follow me to the pond. We got to the pond, and Zara went right in, swimming around for a few seconds. Then she peed in the water again, which caused the gallery to laugh. I just shook my head and smiled. After she got nice and wet, I motioned for her to continue on.

The pond had been located at a perfect spot. After that, she got a second wind. We headed into the area where she'd stopped-to-flush on the pheasants two weeks ago. About 35 minutes into her run, she went on point in some short cover. I started kicking around, trying to find the bird. After checking the whole area near her, I still couldn't find it. Echoing in my head was Melissa's warning that two nonproductive points at a national event meant your dog was done. We had been talking about this at the field trial a few weeks ago. One nonproductive wasn't a big deal, but two was not good. We'd already had one nonproductive. *I have to find this bird*, I thought. This time, I asked the judges if I could relocate Zara. They gave their permission, and I released her. She quickly went on point again in the next row over. Now I could see the bird. She had initially been pointing a long way off. I flushed, and three birds flew a short distance. She handled the sequence like a pro, and we carried on.

There was a scribe riding along with each brace taking notes. He would report the notes at the end of the day on the Vizsla Club of America's Facebook page. According to the scribe, Zara found a bird at 40 minutes, which I have no recollection of. After that, we headed into the woods. We were nearing the end of the course, but we still had a fair amount of time left. I tried to walk slower to eat up some time.

Given the time of day and what I had seen the previous day at the Running of the Veterans, I knew it was likely that the woods held birds. However, the cover was not as thick, which meant they were more visible to the dog, which is not usually a good thing. Sure enough, at 47 minutes, Zara went on point, and, as I hustled up to her, I could see two quail sitting on the ground. She was staring directly at them.

"Wait for us!" the judges called.

"Oh, I'm sorry," I said, slowing down and pausing next to Zara to wait for them to catch up. I was so anxious to flush the birds that I had forgotten about the judges. The next day, the judges would tell me jokingly that I earned the award for walking the fastest. Once they were within view, I kicked at the quail and shot my blank pistol. Zara didn't move a muscle. I gave her more water and released her.

We were almost done. We just needed to get through the next 10 minutes without any errors. I prayed that she wouldn't find any more birds. We walked through the woods to the end of the course. Since we still had time, the judges directed me to continue back to where we'd started. This brought us through another section of woods. Zara continued to run ahead of me. She was definitely staying closer now and not going as fast. But she was still hunting.

Finally, after what felt like an eternity, the judges told me that the hour was up. I called Zara to me and leashed her up. Jane rode up on her horse, and I greeted her with a smile of relief. Zara had made it around clean!

I walked Zara back towards my car, where Chris was waiting. The gallery wagon had dropped him off after the run was over. He congratulated me, and I thanked him for attending. He had only been to two of Zara's other hunting events, so it meant a lot to me that he was there. After a few minutes, I got Zara settled into her crate and said goodbye to Chris, who was headed to DC for the rest of the week.

I walked towards the main tent, and, on my way there, I passed by a group of people who were hanging out along the dirt path.

"Hey!" one of the guys said to me. I stopped and turned to him.

"Hi," I said.

"I don't know who you are," he continued, "but we watched you run, and you did awesome. I've been doing this for 15 years, and I still haven't managed to get a dog around clean at Nationals."

"Oh, thank you," I said, feeling flattered. I introduced myself and chatted with them a little longer. I was happy that Zara had made it around clean, but I wasn't sure how she would measure up to the other dogs. Maybe she had performed like a real field trial dog after all.

The judges watched two more braces on Tuesday before calling it a day. They had completed six braces, and, with only seven more to go, we all assumed that the NGDC would wrap up the next day.

Unfortunately, the weather had other plans. Wednesday started off cloudy with a light rain. This light rain quickly turned into a heavy rain that had no intention of stopping. This was not good news for the dogs, because wet birds don't like to fly. I watched the second brace of the day. One of the dogs that was running was one of the top field trial dogs in the country. I was interested to see how he would run. His range proved impressive, reaching out hundreds of yards in front of his owner. The man walked along at a moderate pace, seemingly unconcerned that his dog was nowhere in sight for minutes at a time.

When it came time for the retrieve, the handler released the dog with a "fetch" command. It looked like the dog did not see the bird fall as he was running around in circles, frantically trying to smell the bird. His handler took several steps forward, yelling, "Fetch! Fetch!" Finally, the dog found the bird and picked it up. He headed back toward his handler, but then took several victory laps around him before the handler was able to snatch the bird away.

Wow, I thought, watching this scene. This was supposedly one of the best field trial Vizslas, and that retrieve, at least by NAVHDA and

Master Hunter standards, was terrible. Maybe he was having a bad day. But, if not, I wondered why his owner hadn't spent the time to clean up his retrieve. I knew that retrieving was not valued as highly in AKC field trials, but it seemed like such an easy fix, which would contribute to a much better presentation. Being in NAVHDA for so long had made me appreciate a solid retrieve with minimal commands and a nice finish.

After this ninth brace, the judges broke for lunch. However, it was raining so hard that they were forced to delay the competition. It poured all afternoon, as we huddled in the tents and our cars, biding our time. I wondered if I should leave and go home, but my gut told me to stay. I had taken the whole week off and had my hotel room until Thursday morning. I might as well stay and enjoy watching the other dogs compete.

Finally, the rain let up enough so that they could restart around 4:30pm. The judges watched one more brace before calling it a day. The NGDC would finish on Thursday morning with the remaining three braces.

The next morning, however, it was so foggy that there was another delay. With the thick fog, it would be impossible to see the dogs when they were on point in the field. After two more hours of waiting for the fog to clear, they could start.

I rode in the gallery wagon to watch two more braces, seeing some dogs get picked up and some finish. I found it a bit surprising that so many dogs had gotten picked up. I felt grateful that Zara had been able to make it around without any major errors. After the final brace was done, the judges quickly convened to finalize the results. One of them needed to be at the Richmond airport at 1pm to catch a flight home.

Chapter 27

Award of Merit

It was finally time to hear the placements. I stood next to the white tents surrounded by the crowd of other Vizsla owners. Even though I had been involved in the bird dog world for close to four years now, I still felt like an outsider. Truthfully, though, these were not my people. They were serious field trialers, professional trainers, and breeders, who had been in this sport for decades. It was different than my NAVHDA community, where, after three-and-a-half years, everyone knew me. I was also one of the youngest participants by far. But I had enjoyed being around them over the past few days, exchanging stories and learning about their dogs.

I knew Zara had done a good job, but this was the second field trial we'd ever entered, not to mention our first national event. I hadn't been to enough field trials to fully comprehend the caliber of dogs we were competing against or how judges typically picked winners. There were plenty of seasoned competitors there, including NGDC winners from previous years. The fact that Zara had made it through the one-hour course without any mistakes was enough for me. We were never meant to be there, after all. A twist of fate, an exceptional performance five years ago, had been the catalyst for a transformation from a pet to a polished gun dog, and me from an ordinary dog owner into a passionate bird dog trainer and competitor.

I tried to keep my expectations in check. I could not be disappointed if she did not win anything. It was truly an honor just to be there. As I waited, I felt myself become anxious in anticipation. I forced myself to take deep breaths to slow my racing heart. It had been a long few days, and I was definitely ready to go home after the awards.

The two judges stepped into the tent. They thanked the participants, the volunteers, and the sponsors. Then the NGDC secretary and the event chair began giving out the awards. In the group of 25 dogs, there was one Award of Merit and four placements. Melissa, the secretary, held up the green Award of Merit ribbon. "This first award is very special," she said, "Because this person is very new to this and just recently earned a Master Hunter title." The woman standing to my right turned slightly toward me. I felt my heart skip a beat.

"The Award of Merit goes to owner/handler Terry Ann Fernando and Zara!" Melissa said, searching the crowd with a smile. Tears crumpled my face, and I shakily stepped forward to accept the ribbon. She handed it to me, and I felt the smooth silk in my hand. It was over two feet long. I stood next to Melissa and the event chair, Pat, for a moment, unsure what to do with myself, eyes swimming. I glanced to my right and saw Jane coming toward me. She also had tears in her eyes.

"I knew you could do it!" she exclaimed with genuine joy. Despite the COVID protocols, we exchanged a hug. I wiped away the tears.

Melissa and Pat continued to hand out the placements. The winner of the NGDC was a male Vizsla who had recently won the AKC Pointing Breed Gun Dog Championship, a similar event that was open to all pointing breeds. The second-place winner was owned by the same man. The third and fourth place awards went to two other owner/handlers. After Melissa and Pat finished, everyone applauded and dispersed to offer congratulations.

It was an unbelievable moment, something I never dreamed I would experience. If you had told me six years ago that Zara would go on to win an Award of Merit at the National Gun Dog Championship, the same event her highly decorated sire had won in 2015, I would have stared at you dumbfounded and laughed in denial. It was unfathomable six years ago. Or even two years ago. These judges and most of the people at this event had no idea what I had gone through to get to this point. They didn't know that Zara showed no hunting desire as a puppy, or that we had not started serious training until she was four. They didn't know the hours and hours I'd spent training her myself, the disappointments I'd experienced, the feeling I'd had over and over that I'd done everything wrong.

But somehow, everything we'd been training for had culminated at exactly the right time, and my effort had paid off in the most amazing way. The stars had aligned, and Zara had put on a performance that I would never forget. Then again, she always knew to bring her A game when the pressure was on. She'd shown that during her first Junior Hunter and Master Hunter Tests. Other dogs, including Colombo, faltered in the face of pressure. But Zara was like that star athlete who always seemed to put on the best performance when it really counted.

Almost immediately after the placements were announced, my phone started pinging with Facebook messages from other members of the Vizsla community, congratulating me. *Wow, word spreads fast*, I thought. I walked back to my car to get Zara for the official winners photo. I reached her crate, and her tail started beating against the side of it as soon as she saw me. Besides being an amazing bird dog, more importantly, Zara was the sweetest, happiest dog I could ever ask for.

"Baby girl!" I exclaimed with wonder. "Look at this ribbon! You are such a good girl." I opened the crate door and clipped the leash to her collar. We walked the short distance back to the tents, and I encountered a woman who I had met at the field trial I had attended a few weeks prior. She had been in the Vizsla world for a long time and had been spectating at the NGDC over the past few days.

"Congratulations!" she said. She paused. "I know I don't know you very well, but do you understand what this means?" she asked. "Earning a ribbon at a national event like this is a big deal," she said, her eyes wide.

"Yes," I said honestly, nodding my head. I had spent more than a year poring over the details of past championship events, dreaming of making it to this point. I knew the significance of it. "It's just so crazy. I got her as a pet dog!" I said, looking at Zara and shaking my head in disbelief. "She didn't start hunting until she was two! I didn't teach her to retrieve until she was five!"

"Wow," the woman said, studying me more intently, as if she could figure out the secret to my success by looking close enough. "Congratulations again."

After taking the photos and saying my goodbyes, I finally got in my car to drive home and shut the door. I let out a deep breath, and tears welled up in my eyes again. After our disappointment in the fall, and the months and months of training, this win felt like redemption. When we had finished Zara's Master Hunter title the previous month, it felt like a foregone conclusion by the time it was over. After all, once she had gotten that first MH pass, I knew she could earn the rest. But this ribbon meant so much more. It was the result of more than a year of building anticipation, and, at times, I felt like entering the NGDC was a shot in the dark. The fact that Zara could hold her own with the top field trial Vizslas was just amazing. I marveled at how far we'd come and felt immensely grateful that this dog had come into my life.

After the NGDC was over, I was ready to take a break from training. We had been hitting it hard for four months, and I was tired. At the end of November, I had finally decided to sell my Honda Fit and buy a new car that suited my dog sports hobby better. I had purchased the Fit years ago when I was single and living in DC. It was a great city car that got up to 43 miles per gallon. But it was not suitable for unpaved roads, and there was hardly any room for gear once both dogs were in it. After acquiring my new full-size Volkswagen Atlas SUV, I had put 10,000 miles on it in the first four months, traveling to train and attend hunting events.

I knew that we'd pick up training again once I felt ready. I still wasn't entirely sure I was going to run Zara again in the Utility Test. However, after talking to several of the participants at the NGDC and seeing how well she did, I figured I might as well try to run her in walking field trials in the fall of 2021. There was the potential of earning a Field Champion or Amateur Field Champion title, but, truthfully, I was more interested in running her just for the fun of it. Finally, after years of training, I would be able to accomplish my initial goal of participating in field trials. Who knew that it would be possible for my spoiled girl to do everything from NAVHDA to therapy dog visits to field trials? She continued to surprise me with her versatility.

By this time, I already had a few people asking me when I would be getting a new puppy. For many performance dog people, a seven-year-old was often considered retired, having earned multiple titles when they were younger. In the show ring, any dog seven and older is called a Veteran. But I didn't think of Zara as old. We were just getting started, really. I knew I would have another Vizsla some day—but as long as Zara stayed healthy, that was at least a few years away. We still had goals to accomplish together, and I owed it to her to give her my full attention a little longer. To be honest, I wasn't sure what I wanted my next dog to be. I would be more selective this time, because I would know going in that I wanted a performance dog.

Should I get one from NAVHDA lines, to have a head start in preparing for the rigors of duck search and retrieve training? I loved being a part of NAVHDA and couldn't imagine not testing with my next dog. Or should I get another field trial bred dog, maybe with some NAVHDA testing mixed in their pedigree? I was beginning to see how fun a field trial dog could be, too. Or maybe I wanted a Vizsla I could show in conformation *and* hunt with.

Also, I had yet to convince Chris that another Vizsla puppy was the right move. He said he didn't want another one, but I countered by reminding him that he got to choose the breeds of our first two dogs. It only made sense that I should get to choose the next.

Finally, puppies are a lot of work, and I was definitely not ready for that yet. I had picked up a lot of training techniques over the years, and I obviously knew way more about bird dog training than I did before I started with Zara, but I still didn't feel like I had a concrete plan for how to go about training my next puppy. Maybe I didn't need one.

But that was the thing. With this next dog, I knew I would put pressure on myself from the beginning, to do everything the "right" way. With Zara, there had been no expectations in regard to titles, so everything we achieved had been a bonus, the icing on a cake that I didn't even know I wanted to make. The expectations on this next puppy, however, would almost be too much.

Chapter 28

Reflecting

After the National Gun Dog Championship, I reflected on everything I had accomplished with Zara and the long road we had traveled since Chris and I picked her up as a tiny puppy. I felt grateful for all of the people we had encountered along the way who had helped us, and knowingly or not, had influenced our course. Zara's breeder Jane had been the impetus for getting us started, and I would forever be thankful for her encouraging nudge. But most of all, I was thankful for the North American Versatile Hunting Dog Association and the Tarheel Chapter members who had become my friends.

Initially, NAVHDA had been a last resort for me, a compromise when I had run out of other viable options. It's funny to think how resistant I was to involving myself in the various tests in the beginning. I had my mind set on field trials, and I was not going to be moved. Little did I know that joining NAVHDA would be the best thing for Zara's bird dog career and my growth as an amateur trainer.

The Tarheel members had welcomed me in the beginning and provided encouragement and helpful suggestions. They had never (save that one encounter with the Pudelpointer owner) mocked my unconventional ways or hinted that training an older dog was something I shouldn't do. Thinking back, it's almost amazing they didn't. And with their gentle guidance and the structure of monthly training days, I had been able to reach heights I never thought possible.

I hadn't realized it at first, but in NAVHDA, I had found my people. Although some of them were individuals that I would not necessarily have been friends with outside of the organization, I felt drawn to them because of our shared interest in our dogs. It took a unique type of person to spend multiple weekends a month sweating in the 90-degree heat to watch their dog do a duck search, or bushwhacking through the thickest cover imaginable to find woodcock, all in the interest of bettering their dog.

After becoming a member, it had taken me a while to feel that I truly belonged, but by the spring of 2021, I was fully entrenched in the Tarheel Chapter and the NAVHDA world. I had taken on the role of test secretary to organize the entries and paperwork for our spring and fall tests, which kept me in direct contact with the executive committee. All of the longtime members knew me by that point and knew Zara's story. After testing Zara for the first time in 2019, I felt like something changed. At the November training day following the test, it was like I had achieved a level of legitimacy. No longer was I an outsider. By trying my hand at NAVHDA's rigorous Utility Test, I had become part of the club.

I enjoyed the family-like atmosphere that NAVHDA cultivated. I have always liked being part of a group. In high school and college, I played clarinet and was very involved in my school band programs. I loved wearing my band uniform and feeling like part of a whole. After graduating, I missed having this kind of group identity. It was harder to find that in the real world. But NAVHDA brought this sense of belonging back to me. I proudly wore my NAVHDA shirt to training days and tests.

After revamping my *Zara the Vizsla* blog to focus more narrowly on dog sports, I wrote a blog post called "What Makes NAVHDA Different?" in March 2020. After being involved in several dog organizations and activities for a while, I was seeing a pattern where participants were getting older, entries were decreasing, and younger people were not stepping up to volunteer.

Except for NAVHDA.

NAVHDA's membership was increasing. Participation in their tests was growing. There were more and more people at every NAVHDA training day I attended. This made me start thinking: why? What made NAVHDA different from AKC Hunting Tests and Field Trials and even unrelated dog sports like conformation?

I think the main reason is because all local NAVHDA chapters host regular training days, where members get together to work with their dogs. The Tarheel Chapter's training days are held monthly for the most part, although there are several months when there is another event (test, fundraiser, etc) instead of a training day. I think this is the key that sets NAVHDA apart. For people participating in hunting tests and field trials, there isn't a similar system of established gatherings. Some local breed clubs may host training days or fun days, but from what I've seen, it doesn't seem to be the norm.

The frequent training days allow people to make connections with others and become friends. Building relationships with people means that you want to see them more and you're more invested in their lives and success.

I remember the first time I volunteered at a NAVHDA test. We had to be there at 6am, and it was pitch-black outside. People were wearing headlamps as they walked around, preparing for the day. Despite the early hour, there was a sense of excitement and purpose in the air. Even though I had participated in many races and triathlons that also required waking up way before sunrise, this felt different. I could feel the community, with everyone working towards a common goal of putting on a successful test and seeing the handlers and dogs do well.

Being in NAVHDA also opened up a lot of opportunities for me that I would not have had otherwise. NAVHDA was where I finally found a place close enough to my house to train on a regular basis. NAVHDA was where I met people who helped me prepare for competitions outside of the organization. And NAVHDA was where I met a friend who would take me hunting for the first time.

Although the Tarheel Chapter had a number of active female members, NAVHDA was still, as a whole, primarily a male-dominated organization. But I am not a girly girl, so I fit right in with the guys. I never got manicures, and I hardly ever wore make-up to training days. I had no issues touching dead birds, and traipsing through a muddy field or a nasty swamp didn't freak me out. I had, after all, spent my childhood playing with pet toads, digging up worms for them to eat, and squealing in delight as they zapped at the prey with their sticky tongues. Summers were spent running around barefoot outside with my sister, inventing our own versions of baseball and street hockey. The soles of my feet would be caked with dirt by the end of each day. Sure, I had played the part of the girly girl in my teens and twenties, because that's what you have to do at that age to fit in. And, more than anything, did I want to fit in. But by the time I hit 30, it didn't matter as much to me what other people thought. Finally, after more than a decade of following the crowd, I started being more authentic to myself.

Being authentic meant indulging in activities that I enjoyed, even if they were "weird" or unusual to other people. Watching movies and keeping up with pop culture, supposedly "normal" pastimes for the majority of society, just didn't interest me that much. Spending time searching for mallard ducks on Craigslist or studying the rules of various hunting dog tests? Sign me up. I reveled in the fact that I had a unique hobby that caused people to raise their eyebrows when I told them that yes, I *was* actually a hunter.

Chapter 29

Discovering My Passion

All of this was because of Zara. She had transformed my life. In the past eight years, I had gone from someone who had no interest in owning a dog to a person who was passionate about dogs, dog training, and dog sports. It sometimes seemed incredible how far we had come. I knew, without a doubt, that our success was the combination of luck, good genetics, and a lot of hard work. There were many, many things I had done with Zara that should have confused her completely and botched any chance of success. But over and over again, she proved able to recover from my mistakes and my sometimes ineffective training. Yes, I had managed to train her to a high level mostly on my own, but I don't present my training techniques as a how-to guide. Far from it. If anything, my training journey with Zara should serve as a guide of what *not* to do with your bird dog. In a lot of ways, I took the hard route, mainly out of ignorance and inexperience.

Thankfully, that's where good genetics came in. Being from solid hunting lines gave her natural instincts and desires that I was able to harness and not mess up too much. Although she didn't show any inclination towards hunting as a baby puppy, I think she had gotten just enough early exposure to birds to build on her genes. She had been on quail at 13 months, 16 months, and 24 months. These sporadic encounters, without a lot of pressure and expectation, had managed to turn her into a hunting machine by the time she went to her first hunt test at 26 months of age.

The rest of it—all the real training, from steadiness to retrieving to obedience—I had undertaken slowly, over the course of several years. Jane reminded me recently that at Zara's temperament test, she demonstrated that she needed to learn at her own pace, and she was also a bit stubborn.

A dog like that may not have done well with a trainer who had forced her to do high-level training at a young age and at an aggressive pace. Letting Zara mature slowly, and allowing ample time for her to learn the tasks, had probably been for the best. It had also led us to build a strong bond.

Spending so much time training Zara had taught me some important lessons. I had finally learned that it was nearly impossible to train a bird dog by yourself, especially as a newbie. Although I certainly tried. But even if I could have, what fun would that have been? NAVHDA had shown me the power of community and how that community can rally around even its most reluctant member.

More than anything, I loved being out in the field with Zara, walking along and watching her work. I loved the process of training her and seeing progress, even if gradual. Time seemed to slip away when I was out there, and I wasn't tempted to check my social media accounts or email. I had her to thank for helping me to find something I was truly passionate about.

In my 20s, I would often think about identifying what my passion was. I'd read articles about people finding their passion and building a career out of it, loving life because they thoroughly enjoyed what they were doing for a living. I wanted that for myself. Sometimes I would brainstorm possible career trajectories, but nothing lit a fire in me. Becoming a creative director at a large design firm? That seemed prestigious, but not extremely appealing. Teaching? Sounded interesting, but weren't you supposed to be passionate about your subject matter? I *liked* graphic design, but after working in the field for several years, I realized that I didn't *love* it.

After we got Zara, I knew I loved having a dog, talking about dogs with other people, and training my own dog. But something was still missing. It seemed just out of reach, but I couldn't quite put my finger on it.

Dog sports were the answer.

It turned out that my passion had nothing to do with graphic design or art. My passion was dog sports—training for, competing in, and discussing everything from hunting tests to conformation shows to dock diving. I especially enjoyed field work. Being involved in NAVHDA went hand-in-hand with this. Eight years prior, before I owned a dog, I would have never seen this coming. But sometimes the best things in life are those that you never anticipate.

Following Gretchen Rubin's mantra of "Choose the bigger life" had turned out to be wise. Deciding to take the leap and train Zara for advanced hunting competitions had opened up a world of opportunity I never knew existed. Amid the monotony of work and daily life, dog sports brought me purpose and excitement. Tests and trials provided concrete goals to work towards with set deadlines. And in Zara I had a willing training partner to whom I felt a sense of obligation. Even though I had initially been hesitant about getting a Vizsla, it turned out to be the best decision I ever made.

Epilogue

September 2023

I n the early morning darkness, I turn onto the grounds of Mingo Sportsman Club, the location of this year's NAVHDA Invitational. Driving carefully over the speed bumps, I follow the line of vehicles onto the property. This slow procession consists of pickup trucks in every size, shape, and color imaginable, along with a sprinkling of SUVs, like mine. Directly in front of me is a dark gray Ford F-150 with a truck cap. The side windows along the back are flipped up to reveal a row of dog kennels. The back of the truck sports a variety of dog- and hunting-themed decals. It's the stereotypical NAVHDA rig.

Seeing these pickup trucks reminds me of my first NAVHDA training day in 2017, six years ago, when I felt so out of place in my small hatchback. Their truck setups, with the rotomolded dog crates, trailer hitch attachments, and drawer systems, holding shotguns, bird bags, and hunting vests, intimidated me. I didn't have any of those things—would I really fit in? All I had in my car was an eager young dog full of untapped talent and a blaze orange vest—the bare minimum.

Now, the sight of the Ford in front of me, and all the others, feels like home.

I belong here. Six short years later and I have it all: a fancy crate, electronic bird launchers, supplies to dispatch ducks, all my accessories arranged in a car organizer. I have five different kinds of ammunition alone, a fact that still bewilders me when I think about the person I used to be. Most importantly, my car contains my dog, who is older now, but still full of talent and desire.

After the National Gun Dog Championship in 2021, I wasn't sure if I wanted to test Zara in Utility again. It seemed like a daunting task, and perhaps one that would end in disappointment for a third year in a row. But eventually, I decided to try one more time to earn a Prize 1. Zara and I spent the summer working on duck search training, trying some new techniques to build her drive. On the day of the test, she did the best darn duck search of her entire life, leaping off the shore, searching around, and then disappearing to the far back of the swamp for the remainder of the time. We earned a Prize 1, scoring 201 out of a possible 204 points. I was thrilled. After three years of trying, we were qualified for the Invitational in 2022.

We had a lot of time before the Invitational, however, so after a two-week break, I decided to enter Zara in the first field trial of the season. Even though the requirements of field trials are quite different from those of NAVHDA, after seeing how well she did at the NGDC, I wanted to give field trials another shot. This was only her third trial, and I was a walking handler, with everyone else on horseback. On day one, to my surprise, she earned third place in the 20-dog Open Gun Dog stake. At the next trial, a few weeks later, she won first place in a 13-dog Amateur Limited Gun Dog stake, earning a 3-point major towards her Field Championship. She put on an incredible performance, ranging further than I'd ever seen and handling two large coveys of birds without missing a beat. Again, I was the only walking handler. Initially, I thought that we could only be successful in walking trials, but apparently that was not the case.

We continued to compete in field trials during the fall of 2021 and the winter of 2022. Zara kept racking up the placements that season. As luck would have it, the 2022 National Gun Dog Championship was once again held in Virginia, at a different location a little closer to Raleigh. Of course, we had to attend. I felt a lot of pressure going into this event, after she won the Award of Merit in 2021. The previous year, we were the unknown underdogs. That was not the case the second time around. Many people approached me with compliments, saying how our reputation preceded us. This added to the pressure, but how could I not be flattered? The past year had brought Zara and me a lot of success, but it wasn't so long ago that I was struggling along, just trying to figure out how to train her.

Before we ran in the championship, I tried to calm my nerves by thinking about everyone who was rooting for us. All of the people I'd met through NAVHDA, through Vizslas, through dog Instagram. I felt grateful to be a part of this bird dog community. On that day, however, an error on my part during the retrieving portion cost us the run. Afterwards, I was very upset at myself, but eventually, I recognized that it was a good learning experience. The mistake exposed a hole in our training, and it showed me what we needed to work on.

Finally, the time arrived in September 2022 to head to the NAVHDA Invitational in Los Lunas, New Mexico. At eight years, eleven months, Zara was one of the oldest dogs participating in the event. I had worried about her age while training that summer, fearing that I might be pushing her too much. Instead, I found that she thrived on the training, including learning the new task of doing a blind retrieve across 100 yards of water. At the Invitational she made me proud, handling the barren desert terrain in the field without missing a beat. However, the setup of the blind retrieve confused her, and she didn't go straight across the water to get the duck. We came very close to passing, and this time, I wasn't as upset as I had been in the past. The failures were starting to get a little easier. I was finally beginning to understand that at these high-level events, there are no guarantees. It doesn't matter who you are or how well your dog had been doing beforehand, there are always things out of your control.

Dogs that don't pass have to earn another Utility Prize 1 in order to go to the Invitational the following year. Originally, I had not planned to try to requalify Zara. I viewed our attempt as a one-time thing since she was getting older. If she didn't pass, I would be content with the fact that we had tried our hardest. But after seeing Zara get so close and watching a dog pass who was twelve years, nine months old, I figured, why not?

The only viable option to requalify her was the Tarheel Chapter's fall test in early December. Part of me didn't believe she was going to get in the water when she'd hesitated in previous years when it was not nearly as cold. I was hoping that her desire for ducks, which had grown substantially in the past year, would override the uncomfortable water temperature.

My assumption proved correct. At the test, she dragged me toward the swamp and entered the water without hesitation. She searched far back into the swamp and found a duck! I was surprised because she had never found a duck in a test before. She completed the rest of the test without error, and we earned another Prize 1. Luckily, this time, in 2023, the site of the Invitational would be a little closer to home, in Bloomingdale, Ohio.

In 2021, my friend Suzann and I traveled to Iowa to spectate the Invitational for a few days and watch several of our friends who were participating. This was my first time at the event, and I was quickly hooked on the energy, sense of community, and daily feeling of tired satisfaction due to the early mornings and long days in the field. I had felt something similar at my local NAVHDA training days and tests, but this was another level. At the end of the first day, we sat among the crowd of people listening to the judges read the scores. There was an older man standing near me, with white hair and a white beard. When the judges announced that his dog had passed, he was quickly surrounded by a small cluster of people, shaking his hand enthusiastically and clapping him on the back in congratulations. He smiled broadly, thanking them, and everyone dispersed as the judges moved on to the next dog. The crowd's attention was now focused on another handler, but I kept watching him. He walked a few steps away from where he had been standing, and I saw the tears well up in his wrinkled eyes. He placed his hands over his mouth and then quickly wiped the tears away. It was almost as if he couldn't believe it.

I watched this with a sense of awe. Here was a man of 70 or so, who, if he was like most of the guys I knew in NAVHDA, was not quick to show emotion. But this moment had broken his stoic facade. Although I hadn't been through the process of training a dog for the Invitational yet, I could sense what this meant to him. This accomplishment, this sense of relief, after a long summer of training with a special dog, had temporarily overwhelmed him.

If the NAVHDA Invitational was the type of event that could make grown men cry, then I wanted in. I wanted to be part of something where the stakes were high, where great effort was required and rewarded, and where the bond between a dog and its handler was the motivating factor behind all of it.

Zara and I now had our second chance, and I was determined for 2023 to be our year. It was not a slam-dunk that fall Ohio day, however.

We started the morning at the double-mark retrieve and heeling portion of the test. Heeling was still a weakness for Zara, and I was not thrilled to begin the day with it. The double-mark sequence ended up being a bit sloppy. But I tried not to get upset about it. I needed to focus on getting through the other parts of the test. I've always found NAVHDA tests to be mentally challenging for the handler and this was no exception. I knew there was a possibility we would not pass for the second time.

The blind retrieve was the highlight of the day. After watching several dogs before us fail to complete the task, I was having flashbacks to 2022. I took a deep breath and lined her up at the water's edge, facing the duck 100 yards away on the opposite shore. I gave her a single command and she charged into the water, swam directly to the duck, picked it up, and headed back. I had put a lot of time into the blind retrieve over the summer, and it had paid off. The field portion also had its challenges, but we managed to make it through. Finally, at nearly 10 years old, Zara became the oldest Vizsla ever to earn a Versatile Champion title, capping off six long years of hard work in NAVHDA.

Driving home from the Invitational through the beautiful rolling hills of West Virginia, I felt like I was soaring. It seemed almost too good to be true, although, if I thought of the monumental effort to get there, the title felt earned. I was content to sit still for the eight-hour drive after nearly a week of getting up every day at 5am, volunteering as a field photographer, and spending every spare moment talking to old and new friends. There were a few phone calls, but mostly I drove in silence and reflected on the past week as well as the almost 10-year adventure Zara and I had been on.

I felt an immense sense of relief. Although passing the NAVHDA Invitational was originally an unanticipated goal, now that I had accomplished it, my journey with Zara felt nearly complete. We would try to finish her field trial titles over the next few months, but even if we couldn't, this dog had already given me more than I could have ever asked for—a passion, a purpose, a community. She had changed my life.

Glossary

AKC – Abbreviation for the American Kennel Club.

AKC Hunting Tests – Noncompetitive events for pointing dogs to showcase their desire and ability to hunt birds. There are three main levels: Junior, Senior, and Master. A dog has to earn several passes to complete a title.

AKC Field Trials – Competitive hunting events that judge pointing dogs against each other. The types of stakes include Puppy, Derby, Gun Dog, and All-Age.

Acting Birdy –When a pointing dog gets in the vicinity of a bird, their behavior often changes. Their tail will wag fast, and they may switch back and forth quickly until they locate the bird.

Back Course –The first portion of a hunting test course. In Senior and Master hunting tests, birds are not shot in this area.

Backing/Honoring –When two pointing dogs are running together in the field and the first one goes on point, the second one should stop when it sees the first dog standing still.

Bird Field – The area in a hunting test where birds are planted and in Senior and Master Hunting Tests, where birds will be shot.

Blank Pistol – A small pistol that makes the sound of a gun when the trigger is pulled, but the end is plugged so nothing is discharged. It is used in field trials and hunting tests when birds are not shot by a gunner.

Brace – A field run consisting of two dogs.

Broke Dog – A pointing dog that has been trained to stand still through the flush, shot, and fall of a bird.

Clicker Training –A clicker is a small handheld device that makes a snapping sound when it is pressed. The "click" is a standardized marker to tell a dog that their behavior is correct. After the click, the dog is typically rewarded with food.

Conformation – A dog sport that judges purebred dogs against their breed's written standard. Only intact dogs can participate in AKC conformation since its original purpose was to evaluate dogs for breeding.

Derby Stake – An AKC field trial stake for puppies from six months to two years old. Dogs are expected to hunt, find birds, and point, but they don't have to demonstrate steadiness.

Divided Point – When two dogs are running together and they both smell and stop to point the same bird.

Electronic Bird Launcher – A metal box that holds a game bird, such as a pigeon. The launcher comes with a remote. When a button on the remote is pressed, the bird is launched into the air and flies off.

Force Fetch – A step-by-step process that teaches a dog to retrieve reliably using some form of pressure.

Gun Dog Stake – A field trial stake for broke dogs over six months.

Heeling – A precise behavior where a dog walks calmly next to the owner's side.

Invitational – NAVHDA's highest level of hunt test, held once a year at various locations around the country. A dog that passes the Invitational earns the title of Versatile Champion (VC).

Junior Hunting Test – The lowest level of AKC hunting tests. Dogs are expected to hunt, find birds, and point. No steadiness is required. Four passes earn the dog a JH title.

Master Hunting Test – The highest level of AKC hunting tests. Dogs are expected to hunt, find birds, be steady to wing, shot, and fall, retrieve to hand, and honor their bracemates without a command. Six passes (five if they have a Senior Hunter title) earn the dog a MH title.

Natural Ability Test – NAVHDA's test for puppies up to 16 months of age. It evaluates dog on various criteria by observing them hunt birds in the field, track a pheasant, and swim.

NAVHDA – The North American Versatile Hunting Dog Association.

Pick Up a Dog – In the upper levels of AKC Hunting Tests and Field Trials, the handler will be asked to leash the dog if it makes a mistake.

Pointing – The instinct of a bird dog to stand and freeze in position when they smell a game bird.

Puppy Stake – An AKC Field Trial stake for puppies from six months old to 15 months old. Dogs are expected to hunt and show their future potential as a field trial dog.

Relocate a Dog – When a dog goes on point and the handler can't find the bird, the handler can release the dog to get closer to the bird.

Running Order – A written list showing the order the dogs will be run in at a field trial or hunting test.

Scout – A person designated by a handler in a field trial to help locate their dog or get the dog back on track if it gets off course.

Senior Hunting Test – The middle level of AKC hunting tests. Dogs are expected to hunt, find birds, be steady until the shot, retrieve within a step or two of the handler, and honor their bracemates with a command. Five passes (four if they have a Junior Hunter title) earn the dog a SH title.

Steady – When a pointing dog remains still in the presence of game.

Stop-to-Flush – When a pointing dog is running freely in the field and a bird pops up unexpectedly, the dog stops automatically.

Temperament Testing – The process of evaluating a litter of puppies around eight weeks of age to see how they respond to various stimuli, their energy level, and their ability to recover from stress. This test helps breeders place puppies in appropriate homes.

UKC – The United Kennel Club.

Utility Test – NAVHDA's test for finished dogs. It evaluates a dog on various criteria by observing them hunt birds in the field, search for a duck, heel, perform a water retrieve, and retrieve a dead duck that has been dragged across a field. Dogs that earn a Prize 1 qualify for the Invitational.

Utility Preparatory Test – A scaled-down version of NAVHDA's Utility Test.

Vizsla Club of America (VCA) – The parent club for Vizslas in the United States. The VCA holds national events and promotes the welfare of the Vizsla breed.

Whoa – A command to get a dog to stop moving and stay in one position until released.

Bird Dog Tests and Trials: An Overview

TEST NAME	OVERVIEW	AGE LIMIT	JUDGING	HOW TO ACHIEVE A TITLE
American Kennel Club (AKC) Hunting Tests				
Junior Hunting Tests	Entry-level test for young or inexperienced bird dogs. Field work only. The dog should point, but steadiness is not required. The birds are not shot, so there's no retrieving.	6 months or older	Judged against a standard	4 passes = Junior Hunter (JH) title
Senior Hunting Tests	Intermediate test for mid-level bird dogs. Field work only. The dog should be steady to shot and retrieve within a few feet of the handler.			5 passes = Senior Hunter (SH) title (or 4 with JH title)
Master Hunting Tests	An advanced test for "finished" gun dogs. Field work only. The dog should be steady until released, retrieve to hand, and back their bracemate.			6 passes = Master Hunter (MH) title (or 5 with SH title)

TEST NAME	OVERVIEW	AGE LIMIT	JUDGING	HOW TO ACHIEVE A TITLE
AKC Field Trials				
Puppy Stakes	Puppy should show desire to hunt but doesn't have to find birds. Field work only. The dog is judged on their running pattern and style and potential as a future gun dog. No steadiness or retrieving is required.	6 months to 15 months	Competitive: judged against other dogs	10 points needed for Field Champion (FC) title. 2 Puppy points can go toward title
Derby Stakes	Derby dogs should hunt and cover ground and must find birds and point. Field work only. No steadiness or retrieving is required.	6 months to 2 years		10 points needed for FC title. 2 Derby points can go toward title
Gun Dog Stakes	Stakes for "finished" bird dogs. The dog must point staunchly and be steady until released. Field work only. Retrieving to hand is required in retrieving stakes, often with a "callback" that is done after the stake is run.	6 months or older		10 points needed for FC title. Additional req. depends on breed: for example, Vizslas need 4 retrieving credits

TEST NAME	OVERVIEW	AGE LIMIT	JUDGING	HOW TO ACHIEVE A TITLE
North American Versatile Hunting Dog Association (NAVHDA) Tests				
Natural Ability Test (NA)	A 3-part test looking at a young dog's natural abilities in the field, water, and tracking. The dog must swim to retrieve two bumpers and track a pheasant, and do a 20-minute field search.	16 months	Judged against a standard	Pass/fail, Prize I (highest), II, or III
Utility Preparatory Test (UPT)	A 4-part test for dogs who are working to become finished. This is a less stringent version of Utility.	None		Pass/fail, Prize I (highest), II, or III
Utility Test (UT)	A 4-part test for a finished bird dog. Includes field work, an independent duck search, heeling, and retrieving. In the field, a dog is run individually and must be steady until released and retrieve to hand.	None		Pass/fail, Prize I (highest), II, or III. A Prize 1 qualifies dog for yearly NAVHDA Invitational
Invitational Test (IT)	A 4-part test for the top NAVHDA dogs, held once a year. Includes a one-hour field run with a bracemate, a 100-yard blind retrieve across water, off-leash heeling, honoring another dog's retrieve, and a double-mark retrieve out of water.	None		Pass/fail. A pass earns the dog the title of Versatile Champion (VC)

If You Are Interested in a Vizsla

As you've probably learned from reading this book, Vizslas are a unique dog breed. They are sweet, trainable, beautiful, and full of life. However, they are also needy, extremely high-energy, and have a high prey drive. If you think a Vizsla is the right breed for you, find owners with adult dogs in your area so you can meet some to see what they're really like. If you decide to get a puppy, please do your research and locate a reputable breeder.

A reputable breeder will breed selectively to improve the breed and follow the standard. He or she will complete the health testing recommended by the Vizsla Club of America (VCA). Both the sire and dam should have Orthopedic Foundation of Animals (OFA) CHIC numbers, searchable on ofa.org.

Consult the VCA's website at **www.vcaweb.org** for a list of reputable breeders.

Acknowledgments

This book has been a labor of love over the past few years, and I am grateful to everyone who has helped me bring it to fruition. Thank you to those who read a draft of my manuscript: Michele Graves, Lamya King, Elizabeth Bracey, Chris Fernando, Emily Shirey, Jane Baker, and Jean-Michel Andreu. Thank you to my editor, Sarah Bodine, for her insightful advice on the genre of memoir and editing finesse. Also, thank you to Sarah, as well as Elise Wright for your guidance in publishing and marketing my book. I always enjoy our creative brainstorming conversations.

Thank you to Jane Baker for breeding Zara and then subsequently being the one to casually suggest that I enter her in a Junior Hunting Test. You gave us our start in a way that was perfect for my formerly hunting-adverse self. My life would be completely different if you had not encouraged us to take that leap. Thank you for your continued guidance and friendship as Zara and I ventured into the field trial world, too.

Thank you to Laura Miller for being such an inspiration with the trails you blazed with Bull, Zara's sire. You set the bar high and showed me what might be possible with my Vizsla girl who didn't like birds as a puppy.

Thank you to the Tarheel Chapter of NAVHDA for welcoming Zara and me into your fold. Joining NAVHDA was truly the turning point in our ability to train for upper-level tests and trials, and the community that came along with it was an unexpected and delightful bonus. I'm especially grateful to the members who were supportive during our first few years: Kyley and Scott Caldwell, Steve and Wight Greger, Nate Davidson, Blake and Stacy Horst, and Mike Neiduski.

Thank you to Emily Shirey for providing guidance and friendship during our initial training phases. Zara would not have a solid retrieve without your help, and it was reassuring to work with someone who embraced low-pressure training techniques. Thank you for showing us how to hunt woodcock. We've had some fun adventures over the years, and I look forward to many more.

Thank you to Blake and Stacy Horst for the training to help Zara learn to honor and to earn a 4 in duck search. That Utility Prize 1, Master Hunter title, and Versatile Champion title would not have been possible without the foundation you helped me lay.

Thanks to Jody Bass for welcoming me as a member of your bird dog club and giving us a place to train on a regular basis. Finding Cripple Creek was like a dream come true after so many years of just making do on the training front.

Thank you to Melissa Thomas for encouraging me to enter the National Gun Dog Championship in 2021. I would not have had the nerve to enter this high-stakes event without your support. You are really the one who was the catalyst to Zara's late-in-life field trial career, and it's been a pleasure to become your friend.

Although I won't be able to name them all here, thank you to my training partners who have helped me time and time again over the years. Putting in the work with you has been the best part of being in this bird dog community: Gretchen Stephenson, Tony Lor, Shoua Lor, Joe and Suzann Novak, Heather Wallace, Wes Everman, Gordon Cashin, Nate Davidson, Mike Salisbury, Grayson Guyer, Ozzie Osborne, and many more.

Lastly, thank you to my husband, Chris Fernando, for being a constant source of support on this journey. It's really all your fault since you wanted the Vizsla originally. ;) Even though hunting is not your cup of tea, you have been my biggest cheerleader through all of this, and I couldn't be more grateful. Good thing you convinced me to get a dog.

About the Author

Terry Ann Fernando has spent the last decade becoming increasingly passionate about dogs, particularly in the realm of competitions and hunting. What began with her Vizsla, Zara, as a beloved pet evolved into a journey marked by remarkable achievements: Zara is now an AKC Master Hunter, a NAVHDA Versatile Champion, and boasts multiple wins and placements in AKC field trials.

Driven by her initial struggles to find adequate resources for Zara's training, Terry Ann is committed to simplifying the training process for fellow dog owners. As a coach, she mentors and guides handlers to succeed in hunt tests and field trials. Her expertise extends to hosting the *Accidental Bird Dog Podcast*, which delves into bird hunting events for pointing breeds.

She lives in North Carolina with her husband and their dogs. Terry Ann continues to share her knowledge and experiences through her website, accidentalbirddog.com.

Online Resources

Website
accidentalbirddog.com

- Blog: Articles about training for hunting events, performance dog health and nutrition, and other dog sports

- Coaching: Information about personalized virtual coaching to help you succeed in hunt tests and field trials

- And more!

Podcast
The Accidental Bird Dog Podcast

- Educational episodes about hunting dog events and competitions that are intended to inspire and encourage other dog owners to do more with their dogs

- New episodes every other Wednesday

- Available on Spotify, Apple Podcasts, or your favorite podcast app

Social Media
instagram.com/accidentalbirddog

facebook.com/accidentalbirddog